THE
GOOD
SAMARITAN
STRIKES
AGAIN

Also by Patrick F. McManus

THE GOOD SAMARITAN STRIKES AGAIN

PATRICK F. McMANUS

HENRY HOLT AND COMPANY
NEW YORK

Published by Henry Holt and Company, Inc.,
115 West 18th Street, New York, New York 10011.
Published in Canada by Fitzhenry & Whiteside Limited,
91 Granton Drive, Richmond Hill, Ontario L4B 2N5.

Library of Congress Cataloging-in-Publication Data
McManus, Patrick F.
The good samaritan strikes again / Patrick F. McManus. — 1st ed.
p.   cm.
1. American wit and humor.   I. Title.
PN6162.M3489   1992   92-10633
818′.5402—dc20   CIP

ISBN 0-8050-2042-X (alk. paper)

Henry Holt books are available at special discounts
for bulk purchases for sales promotions, premiums,
fund-raising, or educational use. Special editions
or book excerpts can also be created to specification.
For details contact: Special Sales Director,
Henry Holt and Company, Inc., 115 West 18th Street,
New York, New York 10011.

First Edition—1992

All stories in this book appeared previously as follows: In Outdoor Life: *"The Worry Box"; "Sighting-In: The McManus Method"; "The Big Fish"; "Now You See Me, Now You Don't"; "The Blundered Buss"; "Chukar Madness" (originally titled "Doing the Chukar Chuckle"); "Cubs" (originally titled "The Cub Scout Blues"); "The Grogan Look"; "The Secret of Goosey Smith's Success" (originally titled "The Secret of Goosey's Success"); "Easy Ed" (originally titled "Easing Around Easy Ed"); "The Good Samaritan Strikes Again" (originally titled "My Life as a Hero"); "Rancid Crabtree and the Demon Bat" (originally titled "Rancid and the Demon Bat"); "My Unsolved Mystery"; "Bring Me One Oscar, Hold the Sarcasm" (originally titled "The Envelope Please"); "The Flashlight Man"; "Snake" (originally titled "An Asp with Class"); "The Kelly Irregulars Learn to Cry"; "Ah, Sweet Poverty!"
In* Glenn Sapir's Hunting and Fishing Travel Guides: *"You Can See by My Outfit" (originally titled "Preparing for Your Outfitted Hunt"). In* Palouse Journal: *"Forget Desire." In* State Magazine: *"The Fly" (originally titled "The Janitor's Journal"). In* Field & Stream: *"Mean Gifts" (originally titled "Gross Gifts"); "Score One for the Pinky" (originally titled "Mr. Taggart").*

Designed by Claire Vaccaro

Printed in the United States of America
Recognizing the importance of preserving the written word,
Henry Holt and Company, Inc., by policy, prints all of its
first editions on acid-free paper.∞

1   3   5   7   9   10   8   6   4   2

CONTENTS

The Worry Box   1

Sighting-In: The McManus Method   9

The Big Fish   17

The Farm   27

Now You See Me, Now You Don't   33

The Blundered Buss   45

Chukar Madness   51

Cubs   61

The Grogan Look   75

The Secret of Goosey Smith's Success   81

Easy Ed   91

You Can See by My Outfit   101

Forget Desire   107

The Good Samaritan Strikes Again   115

Ah, Sweet Poverty!   121

My Unsolved Mystery   131

Bring Me One Oscar,
Hold the Sarcasm   139

The Flashlight Man   147

The Fly   157

Mean Gifts   167

Snake   175

Score One for the Pinky   183

The Kelly Irregulars Learn to Cry   193

Rancid Crabtree and the Demon Bat   201

THE
GOOD
SAMARITAN
STRIKES
AGAIN

THE WORRY BOX

I have this theory that people possess a certain capacity for worry, no more, no less. It's as though a person has a little psychic box that he feels compelled to keep filled with worries. When one worry disappears from the box, he immediately replaces it with another worry, so the box is always full. He is never short of worries. If a new crop of worries comes in, the person sorts through the box for lesser worries and kicks them out, until he has enough room for the new worries. The lesser worries just lie around on the floor, until there's room in the box for them again, and then they're put back in. They're welcomed by the worries that have been in the box all the time: "Hi, guys! Good to have you back. Boy, you should have seen the duds that just left. And they had the nerve to call themselves worries!"

For a while I worried that my worry theory was

flawed. I was talking to an old gentleman who gives every indication that his worry box is empty. Ed's ninety-three.

"Do you realize," I said to Ed the other day, hoping to worry him and thereby gain support for my theory, "that this new federal budget deficit will add another third-of-a-trillion dollars to the national debt? If this keeps on, by the year two thousand, we'll be about five zillion dollars in debt. How are we ever going to pay off a debt like that?"

Ed chuckled and tapped the ash off his cigar. "Beats me," he said. "But it ain't my worry."

"Yeah, sure," I said, "because you're an old geezer. But what about your great-grandchildren? They'll have to pay."

"Don't have any great-grandchildren. Got one that's fair to middlin', but the rest ain't worth a dang. Serve the loafers right if they have to pay off the zillion-dollar debt. Put some grit into 'em."

"Well then, how about the banks and the S and Ls? They're dropping like flies. That has to worry you."

"Nope. Don't have no money."

"Here's a good one. Pollution is eating holes in the ozone layer and within twenty-five years . . . Okay, forget that worry. Let's see. Hmmmm. There's a lot of new sexually transmitted diseases, of course, but I suppose you're in a low-risk group."

"Ain't none lower."

"Yeah, but suppose you went to a dentist who had a deadly disease and . . ."

"No teeth."

"Right. You don't have to worry about your hair catching on fire, either. You could get burglarized, though. How about that?"

"Got nothing to burgle."

I tried for another hour to worry Ed, but without success. He seemed pretty well to have knocked my worry theory in the head.

"I've got to leave now," I said irritably. "Just remember, I'm picking you up at five o'clock tomorrow morning to go fishing."

"Good," he said. "Who's driving the boat, Smoky Joe?"

"Joe can't make it. I'm driving the boat."

"Now *that* worries me!"

I was elated. My theory was still intact. Ed had only one teeny-weeny worry, but one big enough to fill his worry box. He just had a teeny-weeny box.

I, on the other hand, have a very large worry box. My wife, Bun, is one of my major suppliers of worries.

"What did you do with the checkbook?" she asks me.

THE CHECKBOOK! Is that monster loose again? I imagine at that very moment an escaped convict is picking it up off the sidewalk. Maybe he will forge my name and deplete our checking account of every last penny and after he has exhausted all our funds buying dope, he will come to our house, because the address is on the checks, and he and I will grapple with each other, and he will pull a knife and . . . !

"Oh," Bun will say, "here's the checkbook in my purse. Silly me! Now what's wrong with you?"

"Nothing," I say, booting that worry out of my worry box, at least until the next time Bun asks, "What did you do with the checkbook?"

Bun's telephone technique is designed specifically to worry me. The phone rings. Bun picks it up. "Hello. . . . Yes. . . . Nooo! *[Me: One of the kids has done something bad with his car.]* Oh my gosh! How bad? *[Me: It's real bad. Otherwise, the police wouldn't be calling.]* You just never expect these things to happen to you. *[Me: I do.]* When can we see him?" *[Me: Only during visiting hours, when he'll be wearing either a full-body cast or an orange jumpsuit.]*

"So what is it now?" I ask, steeling myself to deal with the horrible emergency.

"Ernie's Garage. Ernie said he fixed the car's oil leak with a thirty-five-cent part. What's funny is that to install it, he had to totally disassemble the car. Isn't that amazing, just a thirty-five-cent part? How lucky can you get! By the way, Ernie says he wants to talk to you about something when you get a chance."

Ernie the Mechanic wants to talk to me? I know what he wants. He wants my house in exchange for totally disassembling my car, that's what he wants. We're about to join the ranks of the homeless!

You see from this example that the old worry about the kid is immediately replaced by a new worry about becoming homeless. I used to pity the homeless; now I am one. And so on. The worry box is always kept exactly full.

Where Bun really excels in worry production for me is on camping trips. It is popularly thought that camping provides a wonderful way to escape from the stresses of modern city life. I myself think this. I can always tell it's time to head for the mountains when I start getting stress cramps in my eyelids. They are quite painful, and cause me to go about for days with a startled, somewhat horrified expression. People coming toward me on the sidewalk look at me and then jerk their heads around to see what's sneaking up behind them. It's an embarrassment, not to mention a major social liability.

Once I'm back in the mountains, though, and Bun and I set up our tent and roll out our sleeping bags, the stress cramps vanish from my eyelids. Soon, I'm drifting into a deep and peaceful slumber, the fragrances of leaf mold and cedar boughs caressing my nostrils. It's nice.

"Was that you?" Bun asks.

"Nope. Probably just leaf mold."

"I mean that snuffling. Did you just snuffle?"

"I don't think so," I reply, trying to recall the characteristics of a snuffle.

"Oh well, go to sleep. It was probably just my imagination."

Yeah, but maybe not, I think. Maybe something outside the tent snuffled. A bird wouldn't snuffle. Squirrels and chipmunks are too small to snuffle. Something would have to be pretty big to snuffle. A deer could make a sound similar to a snuffle but not a true snuffle. Actually, the only animal I've ever heard do a true snuffle is a . . . *BEAR!*

"For heaven's sake, what's wrong now?" Bun asks.

"Eyelid cramps."

Now, here's an interesting aspect of my worry theory. Up to the point where Bun mentions the snuffle, my worry box is neatly layered with worries about the children, work, money, illness, poverty, pestilence, environment, war, the checkbook, famine, etc., each patiently awaiting its turn for my attention. But the instant the snuffle is mentioned, and its source identified as *BEAR*, all those other worries are blasted right out of the box by the sudden inflation of the snuffle worry. War, poverty, pestilence—why, they couldn't even be shoehorned back into my worry box, it's packed so tight with snuffle.

As with most of my worries, the snuffle turned out to be nothing of consequence. The problem with a major worry, though, is sometimes it can produce the very condition that you are worried about.

When I was a kid, I would lie awake all night before the opening day of trout season worrying that I wouldn't wake up at four o'clock so I could be the first one at the best hole on the crick. I kept checking the alarm clock, to make sure it was still ticking. It had awakened me every day for school but it would be just like the treacherous machine to conk out the night before trout season. Every half hour, I checked the tomato can next to my bed, to make sure my worms weren't suffocating. I got up several times to arrange my rod and tackle for a quick getaway. I checked my fishing clothes and boots, to make sure they were all in order, a fairly easy task, because I was wearing them. The night seemed endless. Finally, the clock ticked its way to 3:30. Great! I was going to make it! I closed my eyes in relief. The next time I opened them it was a quarter past ten! *ARRRRHHHHH!*

"The stupid alarm didn't go off!" I screamed at my mother.

"Yes, it did. But you were so exhausted you slept right through it. I thought if you were that tired, you needed the sleep."

"Sleep? Sleep! I needed to go fishing! Maybe there won't be any fish left in the crick by the time I get there. I've missed the best fishing time of the whole season. Maybe . . ."

"Why are you looking like that?" Mom asked, glancing over her shoulder.

"Eyelid cramps."

I was contemplating modification of my worry theory the morning I pulled up in front of Ed's cabin to take him fishing. My conversation with the old geezer had convinced me that as a person grows older, his worry box grows smaller. The box is still always full but it doesn't require so many worries to fill it. By age ninety-three, there's room for only one or two little dried-up worries in the box.

I honked my horn. After ten minutes or so, Ed opened the door of his cabin and headed down the walk. I ate a sandwich, drank a cup of coffee, read the sports page of the paper, and was thinking of taking a nap by the time he got to the car. He seemed in his usual good spirits.

"Why are you always so cheerful?" I growled. "Must be because you have so few worries."

"Nope," he said. "It's because every morning this incredibly wonderful thing happens to me."

"I'm not sure I want to hear this," I said, "but what's the incredibly wonderful thing?"

"I wake up again! Dad-gum if that don't make my day!"

So I guess that's why I put up with the old geezer. It takes so little to please him, and that's one less worry for me.

SIGHTING-IN: THE McMANUS METHOD

There are basically two ways to sight-in a hunting rifle: the calm, logical, and methodical method and the McManus Method. Shooting experts tend to disagree over which is the better method, often posing the question, Who is McManus? The very fact that the question is often posed suggests that these so-called experts are ignorant of my method of sighting-in a hunting rifle. For their enlightenment, as well as that of the ordinary hunter, I have prepared the following article. It is based on my own exhaustive research. Well, maybe the research wasn't exactly exhaustive, but it certainly was tiring.

First of all, you should plan to sight-in your rifle at least a month before the opening day of hunting season. This will give you approximately thirty opportunities to put off sighting-in until "tomorrow for sure." By such skillful management of your time, your sighting-in will be left to the last two hours of daylight on the day before the opening of hunting season. Procrastination is the essence of the McManus Method.

Let's say that your first hunt is on Saturday. You should therefore sight-in your rifle after work on Friday. Limiting the time available for sighting-in your rifle not only produces an agreeable feeling of suspense but simulates the state of excitement experienced when taking aim at your big-game animal. It also gives rise to the confusion, irritability, and exhaustion that typically result from a day of climbing mountains and fighting your way through brush and deadfalls and other obstacles encountered during the actual hunt. Carefully executed procrastination allows you to reap these benefits to the fullest.

Your rifle, shells, and all sighting-in gear should be in the trunk of your car, allowing you to drive directly from the office to the rifle range. By "all sighting-in gear" I don't mean *all* sighting-in gear. You should have forgotten several important items, particularly your spotting scope. The combination to the lock on the gun-range gate is another good one. You may forget any items of your choice, so long as they are not your rifle and box of shells, which I have forgotten on occasion, but that is an excessive handicap and should not be attempted by anyone except shooting experts.

Upon arriving at the gun range, you discover that the gate is indeed locked and that you have forgotten the combination. This produces a nice surge of adrenaline, which is drained off by kicking repeatedly at the concrete gate post and shouting at the lock, which assumes a smug expression, as if to say it couldn't care less that you now have only an hour and a half of daylight in which to sight-in your rifle. You leap back in your car and drive to the nearest phone, not less than five miles away, call your wife, and ask her to hunt down the lock combination and read it to you, which she does, although without the sense of urgency you hoped to induce with high-pitched pleas for haste. While you are entertaining the thought that she has gone out to have her hair done, she returns to the phone with the combination. You then discover you don't have a pencil or paper handy, so you have to scratch the combination on the back of your hand with the little file on your fingernail clipper. Then she says, "I did a favor for you, so you can just do one for me, if you plan on eating any supper tonight. I want you to bring home a few groceries. Stop that whining!" She then reads off a list of nineteen items, which covers your arm from elbow to wrist, and the words *small head of lettuce* actually draw blood, because you notice the sun is already sinking below the horizon.

You now speed back to the gun range, open the gate, drive to the parking area, open the trunk, scoop up your rifle, shells, and gear, and race over to the firing line, where you dump your stuff on a table. You sprint the length of the range to the hundred-yard mark and pin up your target with the file on your fingernail clipper and your tie tack (you're still dressed in suit and tie) because you forgot to bring a stapler, always a good thing to forget, in that it encourages ingenuity in a hunter.

You sprint the hundred yards back to the firing line and get set up on the bench rest and, pausing between wheezes, take careful aim at the bull's-eye, and fire off a shot. It is at this moment you remember that your kid took your $200 spotting scope off to camp with him to use for watching birds and pounding in tent pegs, and you haven't seen it since. So you sprint the hundred yards up to the target to look for the bullet hole. You have to cover the whole hundred yards. Even though you don't see a bullet hole in any of the white areas, there's always the chance you hit the little black bull's-eye dead-on, a miracle that might have put you in contention for sainthood, and you can't determine a bull's-eye hit from a distance greater than fifteen inches, particularly with the light starting to fade. But as luck would have it, you didn't hit the bull's-eye. You didn't even hit the target. Possibly, this is because on the last day of the previous hunting season you bumped the scope while scoring a perfect ten on a triple back-flip from a high log to a pile of rocks. Bumping the scope is the least of your worries on such occasions, so you neglected to check its alignment until later, namely the last two hours of daylight before the present hunting season.

Fortunately, there are no more than four possibilities to account for your having missed the target: the rifle is shooting high, low, to the left, or to the right. If you had brought a large sheet of butcher paper to place behind the target, you would know right off which direction the rifle is shooting. Such practical measures, however, take much of the mystery out of sighting-in a rifle and thereby ruin the guessing game, which is played like this. First, you guess that you missed the target a few inches to the left. So you shoot at the right edge of the target. You then sprint the hundred yards up to the target to see if a bullet hole has appeared on the left side. No bullet hole. You sprint the hundred yards back to the bench rest and fire another round, this time sighting on the left edge of the target. You repeat this procedure—shoot, sprint, check target, sprint, shoot, sprint—until you have exhausted all the possibilities, not to mention yourself. The McManus Method of sighting-in requires that you sprint no less than two miles, and helps you to start getting in shape, which, because of procrastination, you have put off until the last two hours of daylight on the last day before your next hunt. (There's practically no end to the benefits of the McManus Method.)

Let's assume that, after much experimental turning to and fro of the major-adjustment screws on your scope, a bullet hole appears somewhere in the target, say eight inches high and ten inches to the right of the bull's-eye, the shot neatly clipping off the corner of the target and your tie tack. You stick that corner of the target back up with some chewing gum, chewed for just such an emergency, and then stagger back to the bench rest as quickly as possible, trying not to inhale your tie.

At this point, you are ready to fine-tune your scope so that the rifle shoots dead-on at one hundred yards. There are two knobs on the scope, the top one for vertical adjustment and the side one for horizontal adjustment, or vice versa. It is now too dark to see the little incremental marks on the adjustment knobs, so you hold the rifle in one hand and a lighted match in your teeth, while with a dime in your other hand you turn one of the knobs exactly two increments either to the left or right, and sometimes an unknown number of increments, which occasionally happens when your mustache catches fire and flames shoot up your nostrils, thereby momentarily distracting you from the business at hand.

At this point you may wish simply to skip fine-tuning the scope, particularly if you just fired your last shell. All you have to do is remember that the rifle shoots eight inches high and ten inches to the right at one hundred yards. You can compensate for this minor problem when shooting at your big-game animal at a distance of one hundred yards merely by aiming eight inches low and ten inches to the left. Or maybe it's eight inches high and ten inches to the right. It's one or the other, and I'm sure you can figure it out on your own with a little trial and error.

If the big-game animal is three hundred yards away, of course, you must aim twenty-four inches low and thirty inches to the left, which means that, in the case of a whitetail deer, you will be aiming at a patch of ground in front of the animal. If you happen to hit the patch of ground, then the rifle is shooting dead-on, which is the whole purpose of this essay, and you will thank me for having written it. Keep in mind that if the deer is walking to the left at an estimated rate of three miles per hour, you calculate the lead by squaring the fraction $^{24}/_{30}$ and multiplying by 300 minus the combined ages of your children. At four hundred yards . . .

Oh, forget four hundred yards. All this math is starting to give me a headache. Why don't you just stay home on Saturday and watch television? If you're like me, you'll probably need the rest anyway, what with all the exertion required to sight-in a rifle. Any questions?

THE BIG FISH

The Old Man and I had fished fourteen days in a row without taking a big fish. I was not yet an old man, but I was beginning to feel like one. The Old Man also felt like an old man, which was okay, because he was one. He was ninety-two years old. It is wonderful to feel anything when you're ninety-two years old. So the Old Man was happy, and I was miserable.

"Let's call it quits," I said. "We can try for a big fish next year."

"No, we have to keep going until we catch a big fish," the Old Man said. "Besides, I probably won't be around next year."

"Is that right?" I said. "Where do you think you'll be?"

"Either hell or Baja," he said. "You can catch big fish off Baja, and it don't cost you an arm and a leg.

I don't know about hell. Fishing is probably lousy there."

"Can't be much worse than here," I said. "I think all the big fish are gone from the lake."

"Ace told me he caught a twenty-four-pounder yesterday," he said. "There are plenty of big fish left in this lake."

"Ace lies," I said.

"True," the Old Man said. "But he don't lie well. I could tell he was tellin' the truth this time."

"That's too bad," I said. "Now we'll have to listen to Ace brag about that fish all winter."

"It will be an ordeal," the Old Man said. "That's one reason we must catch a bigger fish than Ace's."

"I don't know if I can stand much more fishing," I said.

"You can," the Old Man said. "Now what are you doing?"

"Just cracking the ice off my knuckles," I said.

"Well don't," he said. "It gets on my nerves."

My hands were pretty well shot. After handling lines and tackle and fish every day for two weeks in the cold and the wind and the sleet and the hail, my hands looked like Chipped Beef on Toast. They felt as if the dog had spent the night gnawing on them. Maybe she had. Once I hit the bed at night, all sensation left me. Two bull elk could have fought to the death in our one-room shack without disturbing my sleep. The only thing that woke me was the Old Man's breathing. He inserted pauses in it, probably deliberately, as a joke:

wheeze wheeze wheeze . . . wheeze wheeze. He would work in a pause four or five times a night, and that little silence would jerk me awake in a burst of perspiration, as if a bomb had gone off in the shack. I would lie there alert as a startled deer, listening. After a while, the rhythmic wheezing would start again—not something you'd want to bet money on—and I would drift back to sleep. It's amazing how loud some silences can be. Psychologists probably have a good explanation for the phenomenon.

The morning of the fifteenth day, the Old Man seemed smaller than he had the day before, when he had seemed smaller than he had the day before that. After fourteen days straight of fishing, there wasn't much left of him. He climbed out of bed piece by piece and reassembled himself in the middle of the floor. The little nut-colored knob of a head seemed to protrude from an empty suit of dingy long underwear. For the first time, it struck me that he was actually a small man, much shorter than average, and, now at least, rather wispy of body. I had always thought of him as much larger, the kind of man who caused a room to shrink merely by walking into it. But it had been an illusion. He obviously was a small man, had been one all along. Strange how one's own mind can deceive one, not merely for a moment but for half a century.

"Coffee," he croaked.

"It's bad for the heart," I said, handing him a steaming mug.

"Everything is bad for the heart," he said. "Life is bad for the heart." His hands shook as he drank the coffee. "I had a dream last night."

"I don't want to hear it," I said. "I hate your dreams."

"You'll like this one," he said. "I dreamed that Death came fishing for me with this delicious bait."

I perked up. "What was the bait?"

"Oh, that's a secret between me and Death. It's something *you* would've bit on, though, I can tell you that. But I ignored the bait, just like that big ol' largemouth up at the ponds used to do our baits. So then Death tries another bait and it's even better. And I ignore that. But pretty soon he comes up with a bait even I can't resist, and he hauls me in."

"Hey, that's really a fun dream," I said. "Thanks for sharing it with me."

"Oh, it ain't over yet. So ol' Death scoops me up in his landin' net, and you know, he wasn't a bad-lookin' fella, not bad at all. Looked liked me as a matter of fact."

"Would you go so far as to say Death was downright handsome?" I said.

"Now you mention it, I would. Had a nice personality, too. But he looks at me there in his net, and he starts to frown, like he's disappointed with his catch. I says, 'What's wrong? You got me at last.' Death says, 'Why, there ain't hardly nothin' left for me! You used it all up!' And he throws me back!" The Old Man cackled.

"I didn't know Death was into catch-and-release," I said.

I suspected the Old Man made up at least half of his dreams. I finished my coffee and started putting on my fishing clothes. "You know, Ed, there's something about that dream that really bothers me," I said.

"What's that?"

"I would've expected Death to use better grammar. He not only looks like you, he talks like you, too."

So now we were into the fifteenth straight day of fishing. The lake looked as if it were made of broken slate, a storm congealed in place by cold and reeking of threat. Only fools and madmen would even consider venturing out on it. The lake was already dotted with the boats of fishermen. The season had dwindled to its last five days, which explained why there had been such a large hatch of fools and madmen.

One of my more profound theories is that it's unwise to think too long or too hard about anything you enjoy doing. Otherwise, you will discover that the thing is totally absurd, and the fun will go out of it. That is why I try never to think hard and long about fishing. I prefer to enjoy it as a thing of beauty, a blending of skill and hope and luck and wisdom and an occasional encounter with the unknown and unknowable. Had I not held this theory, I would have raised the question of why two grown men, one old and one not-so-old, would endure the miseries of tossing about on a cold and sullen lake for no greater reason than the feeble hope of catching a stupid fish.

"Big fish bite better in a storm," the Old Man said as I drove the boat into the rising wind.

"Save the fishing lore for Ace," I said. Something fishermen enjoy even more than fishing is the lore of fishing: way you catch the big ones . . . a chop on the water . . . a bronze spoon fished fast . . . a ripple on the water . . . full moon . . . watch the cows . . . a dead calm . . . secret formula . . . off the points . . . *Watch the cows?*

"Head for the mouth of Granite Crick," the Old Man said. "I got a feelin' about the mouth of Granite Crick. Honeymooned there on the beach with my first wife, old What's-her-name. Lived on nothin' but love, sand-hole biscuits, and trout fried in bacon grease."

"Edith," I said.

"What's that?"

"Edith, the name of your first wife. Your only wife."

"Yes, I believe you are right about that. Edith."

"It's seven miles across open water to Granite Crick," I said.

"Same as back then," he said. "Edith didn't seem to mind."

I set a course for Granite Creek. The storm was stretching and yawning and about ready to get up and go to work.

Half an hour later, I was trying to peer through the spray on my glasses as we chugged up a moving mountain of water. As they do in such situations, my senses honed themselves to such sharpness I was able to count not only my heartbeats but the piston strokes of the motor. Both were going at about the same RPM.

"How does it feel to get old?" I asked the Old Man.

"Awful," he said. "Why ask such a dumb question?"

"Because I may not make it," I said. "This storm may save me from old age."

"Pshaw!" he said.

I really hate that word, *pshaw*. It's an old person's word. A young person might say it, but no matter how he tries, can never achieve that infuriating tone of casual disdain that comes so easily to the lips of a geezer.

The storm began to fade as we came within sight of Granite Creek. A half mile out, I hooked a good fish. I could tell it wasn't what the Old Man would call a big fish, but it was good. To me, any fish is good, but this was better than most. Still, it was difficult for me to judge. The fish was very strong and fought hard. Maybe it was not just a good fish but a big fish after all.

"It's a good fish," the Old Man said.

"Can you net it for me?" I asked.

"Sure," he said. "Wait till I get the net before you bring the fish up alongside."

After a few minutes of fighting, the fish began to

tire, and I started working it toward the boat. "What are you doing?" I asked the Old Man.

"Getting the net!" he said irritably. "It's clear back in the stern! What do you think I'm doing?"

"This isn't exactly the *Queen Elizabeth*," I said. I glanced toward the bow. He was still sitting.

When I tried to reach the net myself, the fish broke off.

We listened to the watery slap of waves against the drifting boat, applause from the dying storm for best performance by a fish.

"Sorry about the net," the Old Man said. "In another ten or fifteen minutes I'd have got to it. I'm pretty well exhausted from all that rushing about."

"Rushing about?" I said. "You just sat there."

"To you, I was sitting. To me, I was rushing about. Let's have a sandwich and a cup of coffee."

"Okay."

We let the boat drift while we ate our sandwiches and drank our coffee. "It was a good fish," I said.

"Might even have been a big fish," the Old Man said.

"Really?" I said. "How big of a big fish?"

"Two pounds bigger than the fish Ace caught," the Old Man said.

"I'd guess it to be frve pounds bigger," I said.

"Yes, I'd say easily five pounds bigger."

"Ace probably would have kept a big fish like that, but I released it," I said.

"Yes," the Old Man said. "You are a real sportsman. I even helped you release it."

"That's true," I said. "You did more than your share. Now that I think about it, that fish might even have been ten pounds bigger than Ace's."

"Don't push it," the Old Man said.

The Old Man didn't get his big fish that year, but that's the way fishing goes. Sometimes nothing much happens.

THE FARM

One of my first jobs after college was in a public relations firm. A client would bring in a truth that didn't fit his purpose, and we PR guys would stretch it, twist it, and varnish it to suit his needs. Sometimes we would make two half-truths out of a whole truth, one of our specialties. After a half-truth had been fine-tuned by our technicians, my job was to gloss it over and put some spin on it before packaging. The work paid well and there was no heavy lifting, but for some unknown reason I had trouble sleeping nights. After much soul-searching, I saw there was only one solution to my problem: sleeping pills.

"No sleeping pills," Doc Fishbein said.

"But, Doc," I countered, "I lie in bed all night with my eyes wide open."

"That's because you lie at work all day with your

eyes wide open," he replied. "You can't stand the stress. I suggest you get an honest job."

"I'll look for something else," I said. "But right now I need the money and I need some sleep. So how about some sleeping pills?"

"No pills," he said. "But I'll tell you what I do when I have trouble sleeping. I fantasize about something pleasant until I drift off to sleep."

"That really works?" I said. "How about this?" I told him one of my fantasies.

"Not that pleasant," he said. "Here's my own favorite fantasy for getting to sleep. I imagine that I own this little farm and I wander about doing various chores. I've always wanted to own a little farm, where I could do hard, honest, manual labor in peace and quiet, with the birds singing and the sun shining. In my fantasy, the birds always sing and the sun always shines."

"Gee, I don't know," I said. "I grew up on an actual little farm. I couldn't get away from it fast enough."

"Ah, but this is a fantasy farm," Doc said. "Give it a try."

Strangely, the idea appealed to me. A little imaginary farm would certainly provide a contrast to the stress and strain of my regular job. I decided to give it a try.

When I went to bed that night, my first order of business was to buy the perfect farm. I was pretty sure I could find exactly what I was looking for, too, and at the right price. Pretty soon I found myself hunkered in a barnyard dickering with an elderly farmer who wanted to move into a condo with a pool and tennis courts, and where somebody else mowed the grass and shoveled the snow. I got the farm for a song. Even before we'd signed the final papers, I had drifted off to sleep.

The farm had been allowed to deteriorate, and there was plenty of work to do the next night. Twenty minutes after going to bed, I had reshingled the barn roof, replaced an old bridge across a picturesque creek, cut poles in my own woodlot, peeled their bark, and built an attractive pole fence around half the property, dropping off to sleep before I could fence the other half. The next night I finished the fence, overhauled the tractor, and renovated the chicken house, after which I slept like a log.

By the end of the week, I had planted all my crops and harvested them. I bought a nice Guernsey cow who produced enormous quantities of the richest milk you ever saw but which was also 100 percent free of cholesterol. The chicks I bought Wednesday night were full grown and producing eggs by Friday. I created geese and ducks for the pond I'd dug and stocked with trout. My pigs lolled happily about in their tidy, odor-free pen; my goats wandered about eating only what they were supposed to; and my sheep sprouted wool so fast they needed shearing every other night. The farm was wonderful. My imaginary labors gave me a pleasant sense of exhaustion and relaxation. I slept like a baby.

As with Doc Fishbein's farm, the birds on my farm always sang and the sun always shone. I knew I should imagine an occasional rain for the sake of my crops, but

I couldn't bring myself to do it. One night I noticed the crops had started to wither from lack of moisture. I lay awake for a long while trying to conjure up a rain cloud, but couldn't. I tossed and turned most of the night.

The next day I had trouble keeping my mind on my work and allowed a whole truth to go out unpackaged. My boss was furious.

"What is the matter with you?" he screamed.

"A drought," I said. "My crops are dying and I can't make it rain."

"It's the middle of winter," he said. "There's three feet of snow on the ground."

"Not on my farm," I said.

"I think you've been sniffing the gloss," he said.

That night I went to bed early to see if I could get some rain, and it was a good thing I did. The sheep had gotten out and it took me until four in the morning to round them up and get them back in the pen. I had almost dozed off when I noticed that a bear had knocked over one of my hives—have I mentioned the bees? Exhausted as I was, there was nothing to do but build bear-proof cages around the rest of the hives. I barely had them finished before it was time to go to work.

At the office, I dozed off and started to snore during a business meeting. I awoke with a start and hoped no one had noticed. Unfortunately, my boss was the only other person at the meeting. He had apparently stalked out in a huff, pausing only long enough to tie my shoelaces together.

That night a weasel killed all my chickens shortly

after I had crawled into bed. Then my cow dried up, and a fungus attacked what was left of my wheat crop. I was awake all the rest of the night repairing fences, because my neighbor was threatening to sue me if my sheep ate any more of his oats.

That morning I went into my boss's office and told him I quit.

"I don't blame you," he said. "This racket is getting to me, too. I'm so stressed out I can't get any sleep. Night after night I lie awake staring at the ceiling."

"What you need is a farm," I told him.

"A farm?" he said. "Where would I get a farm?"

"I've got one I'll sell you," I said. "Real cheap, too."

NOW YOU SEE ME, NOW YOU DON'T

I've been sitting here the past few minutes watching a tiny frenzy of sparrows feeding in some decorative bark just outside the window. "Borrriiing!" you say. Well, yes, I'll admit it's not exactly the biggest thrill of my life, but where I live you have to take your entertainment where you can find it.

What fascinates me about these sparrows is that they blend in so well with the bark that if they hold still for a moment, they become absolutely invisible. Of course, they don't hold still for a moment, so their camouflage never totally works, although they do produce the somewhat disturbing effect that little pieces of decorative bark have come to life and are attempting to escape from the flower garden. I contemplate yelling at my wife, Bun, "Run for your life! The bark is alive!" But I've already had my quota of entertainment for the day.

I've always been fascinated by the protective colorations of various kinds of wildlife. How did it happen that certain creatures blend in so perfectly with their background? I've never been able to buy Darwin's theory of survival of the fittest. Let's say that a few eons ago a bunch of pretty, little, bright red bugs show up on a sandy desert, but a couple of these bugs are defective and turn out to be an ugly sandy color. All the pretty bugs make fun of the ugly bugs, but then one day a big flock of sparrows shows up and eats all the pretty red bugs. The sparrows don't even notice the little defective sand-colored bugs, who are sitting off on a dune laughing themselves silly. From then on, all this species of bug is sand colored. That's essentially the survival-of-the-fittest theory. One of the many flaws in the theory is that while the two little sand-colored bugs are sitting on the dune laughing, a camel walks by and squishes them. This, to me, is a more accurate view of life. Darwin was just too much of an optimist.

Now, here is my theory. Some bright little red bugs find themselves on a sandy desert. They take a look at their surroundings and say, "Kee-ripes! We stand out like Yasir Arafat at a bar mitzvah! We gotta do something fast!" So they change to the color of sand, except for a few conceited individuals who remain bright red and get eaten by sparrows. The ugly bugs survive and the pretty bugs don't, which is why we have so many ugly bugs. It makes sense.

Consider the hairy mammoths. At one time they lived in a tropical climate and were simply plain old bald mammoths. Then it started to get cold. The bald mammoths told themselves they had better start becoming hairy if they wanted to survive the cold, so they became hairy. They didn't survive anyway, but at least they made the effort. This has great philosophical significance for us humans, and I wish I could figure out what it is. I mentioned my theory to Bun, but she said I'd better knock off watching sparrows for a while. Few wives have any aptitude for science.

Even more fascinating to me than the various camouflages of wild creatures are the assorted disguises that nature has concocted. There is, for example, the moth with the two large, mean-looking eyes on the tops of its wings. I had a grade-school teacher with eyes like that, and nobody messed with her. So I know that this moth is onto a good thing.

I once read about a worm that could curl up on top of a stump and disguise itself perfectly as a bird dropping. That may seem a little extreme, but, hey, you do what you have to do when it comes to survival. I've been in situations where, if I could have disguised myself as a bird dropping, I wouldn't have thought twice about it. In junior high, there was this kid, Raymond, who was always trying to beat me up. Let's say Raymond comes swaggering down the street looking for me. "You seen McManus around?" he asks one of his henchmen. "Naw," the henchman replies. "But here's something interesting. I just saw a bird dropping run up that alley."

When I was a boy, we used to have a game warden in our county who had mastered the technique of blending in with his surroundings. His name was Sneed, and he had the uncanny knack of showing up at exactly the time and place of a game-law violation. A poacher would shoot a deer out of season and decide to hide it behind a tree, and the tree would turn out to be Sneed.

I never violated the game regulations myself, except one time when I gave into an irresistible compulsion to fish the town's water reservoir. The fishing was great. Like other criminals, as soon as I broke one law, I didn't mind breaking another, and caught more than my limit of trout. I probably would have started robbing banks next, except my ten-year-old nervous system was shorting out from worry about Sneed. Still, there was no way he could sneak up on me, because I had a clear view of the only approach to the reservoir. Sneed fooled me, though. He made himself invisible until he was within an arm's length of me. If my tennis shoes hadn't been laced tight for a fast getaway, I would have jumped right out of them. The game warden apparently figured he had punished me enough by scaring five years off my life, because he let me go with only a stern lecture. I saw at once that I possessed neither the nerves nor the aptitude for crime, and from then on went straight.

I'm pretty good at blending in myself. Most of the

time I was in school, I disguised myself as an empty chair in the back row of classrooms. I got so good at it that occasionally I was marked absent when I was there. On the rare occasions that I thought I knew the answer to a question, I would shoot up my hand. The startled teacher would nod in the direction of my chair, and I would give a wrong answer. Even a wrong answer would be worth some points, though, because any response at all from an empty chair impresses most educators. Sometimes I would flunk a course, but my chair would pass with a D-minus.

My good friend Albert also sat in the back row and had mastered the technique of making himself invisible. The only difference between me and Albert was that he was a genius. At our graduation from high school, he gave the valedictory address, but nobody could see him. His mother was so embarrassed that she made herself invisible too. It ran in the family.

In college, some of my friends and I raided a dormitory at a neighboring university on the eve before the big football game. We didn't really want to raid the dorm, but it was part of the tradition between the two schools. One reason we didn't want to raid the dorm was a rumor that if we were captured, a car would one day pull up in front of our student union building at noon and expel the captives, wearing only a crudely painted version of the enemy university's emblem. It's pretty hard to blend into a crowd when you're stark naked. Strolling casually along with the flow of pedestrians doesn't cut it. Whether or not the rumor was true, capture during a raid was not pleasant to contemplate.

Late at night, my three associates and I found ourselves on a seek-and-steal mission deep in the heart of the enemy dorm. Our target was the dorm trophy case, from which we planned to remove a few cherished items and replace them with a ransom note, even though we intended to return the trophies after the Big Game.

As the leader of the raiding party, I assigned myself the job of lookout while my three companions worked their way toward the trophy case. Strangely, the enemy dorm anticipated our raid, even though such a thing had only occurred every year for the past half century. A patrol roamed the halls to guard against an attack. Suddenly, a marrow-freezing shout rang out: "It's a raid! Get 'em!"

All around me doors flew open, and outraged enemy students poured into the hall. I was trapped! At that moment, I saw my three companions beating a mad retreat for the nearest exit, three floors down and ten miles distant. My only hope was to blend into my surroundings, made all the more difficult by the fact that I was the only one around fully clothed, drenched with cold sweat, and quaking like an aspen in a high wind. "There they go!" I croaked loudly. "After 'em, boys!" With a minimum of remorse, I led the enemy charge after my three friends, clattering down stairs, racing down halls, and shouting, "Somebody get a rope!"

When the posse burst out of the dorm, the three escaping raiders were scorching earth scarcely ten yards ahead of us. They leaped into the getaway car and took off, obviously giving little thought to the fate of the fellow raider they had abandoned. The posse, moaning with disappointment, slowed to a stop—all except for its charismatic leader, who continued in hot pursuit of the getaway car. "Hey, man, give it up!" a voice from the posse called after him. "You can't catch 'em now!" But the leader streaked on in relentless pursuit of the villains, never slowing his pace until he had vanished into the cover of darkness. It was one of the best jobs of blending I've ever pulled off.

After I graduated from college, I went to work for a newspaper. The city editor would say, "I need somebody to cover the planning commission meeting tonight." As he scanned the newsroom for available staff, all the other reporters would make themselves invisible. Up to that moment, the newsroom had been filled with cigar smoke, the clatter of typewriters, and a cacophony of shouts, babble, and raucous laughter. Silence would fall on the room like a rock. The cigar smoke would waft away to reveal only the city editor and me. "You're it, McManus," he would say, after which the newsroom would roar to life again. It wasn't long before I could make myself just as invisible as the veteran reporters, and I've kept in practice ever since.

Making yourself invisible comes in handy for avoiding panhandlers, street mimes, subway gangs, tavern toughs, car salesmen, and wives looking for someone to hang a picture. I'm so comfortable with being invisible that sometimes I forget to become visible. I think clerks, waiters, and taxi drivers are merely ignoring me for their own amusement, but then I realize I've forgotten to make myself visible. I've run into some other problems with invisibility, too.

When I'm wearing my camouflage hunting clothes, you need one of those high-tech body-heat sensors to detect me. I become nothing but slightly thick air. It can be embarrassing, though. I was walking down a mountain road in my camos last fall when I heard a car coming. To check out my invisibility, I backed into some brush at a turnout to let the vehicle pass. It didn't pass. It pulled into the wide spot and two matronly ladies got out. I now realized that if I suddenly emerged from the brush, I might frighten them, so I remained still and silent, hoping they didn't have a body-heat sensor with them.

"Good heavens, Hazel," one lady said to the other. "I would think you could at least wait until we get to a gas station."

"Well, I can't!" the second lady snapped back, peering up and down the road. "I shouldn't have drunk that third cup of coffee!"

I thought about growling, "Hey, lady, this ain't a public restroom, you know!" On the other hand, I realized the woman was in no condition to be startled by a bunch of tree bark speaking to her from ten feet away. The tree bark chose to avert its eyes, and presently the ladies sped away, obviously more at ease from the pause in their travels, which was more than could be said for the tree bark.

A couple of years ago, I was hiking along a remote mountain trail in my camos and sat down to rest and gaze out over the valley below. Presently, another hiker came down the trail. I assumed that he saw me sitting there, because he looked in my direction several times. He stopped a few feet away from me and, without a word of greeting, turned to gaze out over the valley. At any moment, I expected him to say something to me like, "Wow, that's really beautiful, isn't it?" But he didn't. He just stood with his back to me and gave not the slightest indication of recognizing my existence. Well, I thought, if you want to be rude, I can be rude, too. I won't speak until you do. I sat there irritably contemplating my belly button, which was covered with camouflage. Realization struck. I blended so perfectly into the background that, even though the hiker had looked right at me, he hadn't seen me! Now, he was standing on the edge of a thirty-foot cliff, so close I could reach out and push him off.

I've had a lot of experience with predicaments, so I had no trouble recognizing this as one. What should I do? If I sat there and said nothing, the fellow might turn around and suddenly see me sitting there. Perhaps he would leap to the conclusion that I was sneaking up on him and reflexively run me through with his walking stick. Or the leap he made might be backward into empty space. A slight sound from me could prove devastating to one or the other of us. The situation was beginning to stress me out. A sharp limb I hadn't noticed before attempted to perforate my back. A major cramp gripped one of my legs with such intensity I could barely restrain a groan. In an effort to relieve the cramp, I eased forward into a posture that I suppose could easily have been misinterpreted as a crouch. Then a maddening urge to cough possessed me. For those reasons, I may have been looking a little wild-eyed and possibly even slightly demented at the moment the hiker turned and gazed directly into my face. I tried to say something by way of casual greeting but only succeeded in releasing my pent-up cough, which came out as a sort of maniacal bark. There was a two-second delay in the hiker's response.

I eased my back off the sharp branch. After massaging the cramp from my leg, I got stiffly to my feet and picked up the hiker's walking stick from where it had clattered onto the rocky trail. The stick was a store-bought job, no doubt fairly expensive. If I ever saw the hiker again, I would return his stick, but that possibility seemed remote. I assumed, quite correctly I believe, that any effort on my part to run after him waving his stick would only encourage an acceleration in his pace, which, to judge from the sounds below, was already causing him considerable difficulty in negotiating the sharper switchbacks on the trail. I hoped he wouldn't report me to the sheriff. Law-enforcement officers in the area would instantly recognize the M.O. and nail down my identity within minutes. They already consider me something of a nuisance, if not an outright troublemaker.

Uh-oh, here comes Bun, with that expression on her face that says "a few little chores." Time to make myself invisible. *Fast!*

THE BLUNDERED BUSS

Having pretty well exhausted my interest in quantum physics, which took the better part of three minutes, I recently turned to a much more fascinating subject for pondering: the firsts of my life, such as first kiss or first fish. Oddly, I haven't been able to extract my first fish from the mists of time, but memory of my first kiss leaped forth with agonizing clarity.

Perhaps what makes my first kiss so memorable is that it was conducted more as a scientific experiment than as an act of adolescent lust. I simply wanted to determine what kissing a girl felt like, nothing more. My interests at the time centered mostly on guns and hunting, and I tried to transfer my knowledge of shooting to the act of kissing, the similarity in these activities being that in each there is a target you're supposed to hit.

The situation was this. My cousin Buck showed

up at my house to request a favor of me. Buck was several years older than I and possessed a driver's license along with, and more importantly, a car. He would on occasion interrupt the car's basic purpose as a vehicle for his amorous pursuits and use it to take me hunting and fishing. The car was his main hold on my loyalties, other than brute force. The reason he had singled me out for the favor was that someone—I didn't know who—had started a rumor that I was quite a ladies' man and that most of the girls in my freshman class at Delmore Blight High were absolutely crazy about me. The person who had contrived this mischief had even suggested that I was a great lover. He had even invented numerous fictional anecdotes in support of that reputation. I realized, of course, that the person who had started the rumor was probably a shy and insecure boy totally lacking in experience with the opposite sex, a lad not unlike myself. I could only sympathize with the rumormonger, and saw no reason to cause him embarrassment by denying the rumor, much as I would have liked to when I heard the favor Buck requested.

"Hey, lover boy," he greeted me. "Guess what you're doing Saturday night."

"Going to a movie," I said. "A Randolph Scott Western. I can't miss it."

"Yeah, you can. Listen, I got a big favor I need to ask you. You know my new girl, Velveeta? Well, her cousin, who's about your age, maybe a little older, is coming to town, and Vel insists that she hang out with us. So I need you for the cousin. I figure I'll take 'em

out for Cokes and burgers, and then I'll pick you up
on the way out to the gravel pit."

No, not the gravel pit! For years I had lived in
terror of one night finding myself lured to that infa-
mous hole. The gravel pit was the local lovers' lane, or
in this case, lovers' pit.

"Hey, the gravel pit," I yelped. "You don't have
to twist my arm to get me to go to the gravel pit!"

"That's better," Buck growled. "If you'd just said
so first, I wouldn't have had to twist it."

Thus it was that the following Saturday night I
found myself on the opposite side of a backseat from a
girl who looked like a movie star. She had blue eyes
and tawny hair and an actual figure, and she was darting glances at me that sophisticated young women re-
serve only for freshly squished worms on a wet
sidewalk. The small part of my mind unparalyzed by
terror deduced that this was going to be a long and
harrowing evening at the old gravel pit. I made a men-
tal note to mention to Buck the next day the anguish
he had caused me. Then I'd kill him.

Scarcely had we arrived at the gravel pit than Buck
and Velveeta began exchanging passionate kisses. I
made a quick study of Buck's technique, never before
having had the opportunity to observe passionate kisses
at close range, so close in fact that the sounds emanating
from the front seat reminded me of those made by
toothless Old Man Crawford slurping up a bowl of
noodles. Never before had I put Old Man Crawford
and romance in the same thought, which says something about the stress of the evening.

Although I appeared outwardly calm and casual, despite the loss of all feeling in my extremities, my mind had recovered from its paralysis and now ricocheted about the inside of my skull in wild panic. To rein it in, I started to pretend to myself that this girl was merely another quarry to stalk. I would simply apply the same psychology I used to fend off buck fever, or in this case, doe fever. I was by no means totally opposed to kissing the girl, because I had long wondered what it would be like. It would be interesting to analyze the sensations, coldly and objectively, as a scientist would do with any experiment.

Despite my painful ignorance about all matters related to the opposite sex, I nevertheless realized that it would be uncouth of me to treat a girl as a mere science project. Before attempting to conduct the experiment, I thought I should first get to know something about her as a person, such as her name, for instance. My attempt at engaging her in preliminary casual conversation was not helped by the noodle-slurping sounds emanating from the front seat.

"By the way, what's your name?" I inched across the seat toward her, beginning my stalk.

From the front seat: *slurp smack slurp slurp smack.*

"Opal."

"So, how about them Yankees, Opal? Won three in a row." Inch inch.

Slurp smack slurp slurp smack.

"Yeah."

Slurp smack . . .

"Uh, hot lunches at our school are really terrible.

I bet they are at yours, too. You like noodles?" Inch inch.

Slurp smack . . .

"Yeah."

As I drew within firing range of her moist scarlet pouting lips, Opal suddenly tilted back her head and closed her eyes. For a moment I thought she had dropped off to sleep, but then realized she had somehow divined my intent, and even approved of it, if only as a means of killing time. Cold sweat gushing from every pore, I took a deep breath and poised myself for the shot, finger tightening on the trigger, so to speak. Then I made a stupid error: I shut my eyes! Blindly I went for the target, only to discover too late that I had miscalculated the trajectory. My dry, puckered, quivering lips closed not on a soft, more or less receptive mouth but on a hard, unyielding protuberance. Startled by the unexpected sensation, I popped open my eyes to reorient myself and discovered I was kissing the bridge of Opal's nose! Cripes! Two wide and indignant blue eyes stared directly into mine from an inch away, rather disconcerting, I must say.

So back to witty conversation. Presently, Opal closed her eyes and tilted back her head once more. As I pondered whether to run the experiment again, with my eyes open, a tiny snore escaped her lips. I knew then that I had no great talent as a lover, or as a witty conversationalist either, for that matter, and in the future would concentrate only on stalking game possessed of either four legs or feathers. Still, a first kiss is a first kiss, even a blundered buss.

CHUKAR MADNESS

You can't imagine how thrilled I was when my boss phoned from New York and asked me to guide him on a chukar hunt in the wilds of Oregon. Not only would I have the opportunity once again to practice my guiding skills, but I would be able to impress an important outdoor editor, one Clare Conley, with my considerable knowledge of woodcraft.

"One more thing," Conley said. "I'm bringing my son Ted. He just graduated from college and has a break before he starts law school. He's never hunted in the West before, and I thought this would make a nice little vacation for him."

"Fine," I said.

I was a little surprised that Conley wanted to hunt chukars. I had hunted chukars for twenty years and more and still nursed the hope of someday shooting one. They are a mean and sadistic bird. A few decades ago a band of outlaw chukars was run out of Asia Minor and sneaked into this country. They took up homesteads on the steepest, driest, rockiest country they could find in the West, and began to multiply, and even add and divide. They're smart. Pretty soon hunters, not knowing any better, started hunting them. Many were crippled and some even killed, and occasionally one of them even got a shot at a chukar.

It is chukars' standard practice to lure the hunter up a steep incline by milling about in full view, giving the impression that they have no more wits about them than a flock of chickens. The hunter starts up the hill after them. When he is almost in shooting range, they begin running uphill. The hunter runs after them. The head chukar sets the pace. "Slow up a bit, folks," he tells the others. "The hunter is getting discouraged. Let him close the gap by another ten feet. Good! Now pick up the pace!" In this way, the hunter is teased into running at full tilt all the way to the top of a steep, rocky, treacherous mountain, in the belief that the next agonizing step will at last bring him within shooting range. If he stumbles and falls, the chukars stop and wait for him to get up, dangling the carrot of hope before his eyes, to lure him on. Then they take off again. When the chukars reach the top of the mountain, they leap into the air and glide back to the bottom, doing their chukar chuckle as they pass over the tattered remains of the hunter, whose heart and lungs have burst but who still blasts vainly away at the descending flock. That is the essence of chukar hunting. Only a madman would take it up as a sport.

"So, ready for a little chukar hunting, are you?" I greeted Conley at the airport.

"Am I ever!" Conley said. "I live from one year to the next to hunt chukars."

"Yeah, me too," I said. "Nothing I enjoy more than chukar hunting."

Conley introduced me to Ted, a tall, handsome young man who seemed perfectly sane. I noticed that mention of the word *chukar* did not bring a maniacal glint to his eyes, as it did to his father's. This was a good sign. It seemed likely that Ted and I could lounge about the car and swap stories, while the senior Conley chased chukars up mountains.

The hunt started off badly. Before long, we were lost and found ourselves climbing aimlessly up steep inclines. Conley began ranting about my sense of direction and guiding expertise.

"Surely you've been lost before," I countered.

"Yeah, but not in an airport parking garage!" Conley shouted, dragging his duffel bag and gun case up a flight of stairs.

"Look for a red Jeep Cherokee," I directed. "It's got to be here someplace."

"Half the cars are red Jeep Cherokees!"

"I know," I said. "That's why you need a guide. Without me, you'd never find the right car."

Scarcely an hour later the car was found, and we were zipping down the highway toward Oregon. Conley relaxed into a mellow mood and began to talk hunting. Ted snoozed sensibly in the backseat.

"I read about this frog in Africa or someplace,"

Conley said. "It wakes up only about two months a year. It eats, drinks, and mates almost continuously for two months and then goes back to sleep. Sort of the ideal life, if you ask me."

"If you're a frog," I said.

"Shut up and listen," Conley said. "That frog has given me an idea. I've been trying to find a way to work more chukar hunting into my life, and I think I've got it—cryogenics!"

"Terrific idea, boss!" I said. "I wish I'd thought of it." The man was truly mad.

"Just as I expected, you've never heard of cryogenics. What it is, you get yourself quick-frozen and years and even centuries later, you get thawed out and you're just as good as when you were first frozen."

"Yeah, except for a little freezer burn! Ha!"

"Can the sarcasm. So my plan is this. I get myself frozen right at the end of a chukar season. The only way to get in shape for hunting chukars is by hunting chukars, and that's when I'd be in top shape. Then I get thawed out just before the next chukar season opens. That way I've used up only a couple of months of my life doing what I love to do, hunting chukars. I could work six chukar seasons into what otherwise would amount to a single year of life."

"Gee, boss, maybe I could help out," I said. "I could be in charge of thawing you out just before each new chukar season."

"No, you're too absentminded. I could be frozen for years before you remembered to thaw me out. I'd have some kind of computer set to do the thawing."

"Maybe we could try it with me just the first time and see how it works out."

"Absolutely not! Don't even think of it. Anyway, I get thawed out, and I ask around how the chukar population is that year. If it's down, I just get frozen back up till the next year. Maybe I'd even have my dog frozen with me."

"He'd like that, I'm sure," I said. "While you're at it, why don't you have a few coveys of chukars frozen right along with you?"

"No, that wouldn't be sporting. You have to leave the element of chance in hunting. Otherwise, it's no good."

"So why not let me be in charge of thawing you out?"

"There's such a thing as too much chance," Conley growled. "Where are we, anyway?"

"Beats me," I said. "I was concentrating on driving."

We eventually arrived at the hunting ground, all of it pretty much vertical and covered with loose rock, slick grass, squatty brush, and irritable rattlesnakes.

"Beautiful!" cried Conley. "Did you ever see anything more beautiful? This is the best chukar country I've ever seen. From now on, we'll have to hunt this every year. Is that great or what?"

"Great," I said, even though it was mostly what.

We bivouacked that night in a Pendleton hotel and set out before dawn on our first hunt, which started off badly.

"I know I parked it around here someplace," I

explained. "But maybe it was in a similar parking lot on the other side of the hotel. Look for a red Jeep Cherokee."

"Ye gods!"

By the time we reached the hunting grounds, dawn had not only cracked but oozed down into the narrow creek bottom, where sensible men could hunt pheasants and quail to their heart's content, without so much as breaking into a sweat. Above us rose high, steep, loaf-shaped mountains from which drifted down the sardonic chuckles of chukars.

"Just listen to that," Conley said. "Music to my ears. And there's a flock of them!"

I glanced up. Sure enough, on a rock ledge fifty yards up the mountain, an insolent mob of chukars stared down at us. We leaped out of the car and charged up the grade after them. It's Conley's theory, as yet unproven, that if you charge madly at chukars, they will be startled into flight and you can then shoot them in a sportsmanlike manner. The chukars know this. The mob milled about until we were well within shooting range. Then the head chukar said, "Okay, guys, we've got them on the run. Remember, nobody flies, right? They're almost here. Now, everybody run uphill!"

We chased the chukars all the way to the top of the mountain. Then they leaped into the air and soared down to a ledge on the next mountain over. Conley and Ted watched them sail away, while I beat on my chest with a large rock in an effort to get one or more vital functions operating again.

"Gosh, Dad, they got away," Ted said, his tone of

surprise confirming that he had never before hunted chukars.

"That's what they think," Conley said, chortling. "I saw right where they landed. What we'll do, I'll walk straight down this mountain and come up below them. Ted, you swing around over that high saddle and come in from the right. Pat, you go back down to the road, climb halfway up that mountain and come in from the left. We'll have them surrounded."

"But won't they just run to the top of that mountain?" Ted said.

"If they try to run, we'll charge them and make them fly."

"Gee, I don't know about this chukar hunting," Ted said, wiping his face with his sleeve.

"You'll catch on to it," Conley said. "It takes a while to get in shape for chukar hunting. That's when it gets to be great fun. You'll see."

Lies, all lies, I thought. You wouldn't think a man would lie to his own son, unless it was about something important, like fishing. Ted obviously was a sane, sensible young fellow, displaying a wisdom way beyond his years. With both Ted and me aware that chukar hunting was one of the more severe forms of insanity, that would mean we could outvote the senior Conley two to one and go hunt flatland birds instead. The difficulty would be getting the decision put to a vote.

Conley and Ted strode off to surround the chukars, and I plodded back down the mountain. When I got to the Jeep, I dug into the cooler and grabbed an ice-cold cola and a sandwich. Then I drove up a game trail to the foot of the next mountain. I got out and struggled fifty yards or so uphill, until I found a soft rock unoccupied by a rattlesnake, and sat down behind a bush to enjoy a little nourishment and refreshment. Then I settled back for a nap. This was my preferred method of hunting chukars. Scarcely had I tilted my hat over my eyes, however, when two shots rang out above me on the mountain. These were followed by two more, only farther away. Shots are always a bad sign, when you're engaged in my preferred method of chukar hunting.

Presently, I saw Conley striding down the mountain, a big smile on his face. I leaped up and pretended to be striding in from a different direction.

"Any luck?" I called.

"Got a double!" he yelled back.

So, just the kind of luck I had expected: bad. There'd be no stopping Conley now. Then Ted came slogging down off the mountain. He was frowning. Good. A sliver of hope remained.

But as Ted approached, a big grin spread across his face. He reached in his game bag and pulled out a chukar. What a disaster! Even from several yards away, I could detect the glint of chukar madness in his eyes. It had to run in the family.

Now I was doomed to chukar hunting for a whole week. And the next year! And the year after that! Forever!

"Boss," I said, "let's discuss this cryogenics idea of yours some more. I like it. You and Ted and your dog get frozen, see, and I thaw you out just before chukar season. I could mark it on my calendar. How does that sound, my marking it on the calendar?"

"Terrible. Now where did you park the car? I heard you driving it. I'm dying for an ice-cold soda."

"Well, it's right over . . . uh . . . Is that north or east? Let's see, I think I came up that trail, but it may be the one over there."

CUBS

I like to think I was just as good a Cub Scout as the next guy, the next guy being Grover Finch, who was about as miserable a Cub Scout as ever tied a granny knot and called it square.

Our den could boast of boys clearly cut out for the scouting life, but I wasn't one of them. Neither was Grover. He dropped out of Cubs shortly after the strange incident at Camp Muskrat. I think he may have received a dishonorable discharge, but I don't know for sure.

It was Grover who taught us a lot of good stuff not covered in the Cub Scout manual. He showed us how to tie a hangman's knot and also demonstrated how it worked, slipping the loop over Terry Greer's head and pulling it tight. Terry got into the act and made a strangling noise, then flopped on his back on the floor of our den mother's living room, his tongue sticking out six inches and his eyeballs protruding comically. It was wonderfully realistic, particularly because his tongue was all purple from a grape sour ball.

Mrs. Slocum, our den mother, came in from the kitchen about that time carrying a tray of hot cocoa and cookies. Her eyes protruded even more than Terry's. Then Grover, never one to leave well enough alone, said, "Caught him stealin' cattle, ma'am, so we strung him up." Mrs. Slocum released a screech that sent her cat halfway to the ceiling and then out of the room without ever touching the floor. Displaying an athletic prowess we never suspected, our plump, matronly den mother bounded over a wing chair and a coffee table with the agility of a startled gazelle, dropped on poor terrified Terry with all fours, ripped the noose off over his head, and pumped down on his chest so hard that the sour ball shot three feet into the air.

As soon as we got Mrs. Slocum calmed down a bit, a couple of us pried her cat off the kitchen wall and gave it to her to pet, just to show we were trustworthy, loyal, and helpful. The only real damage was cocoa stains that never did come out of our Cub Scout shirts. Cookies had sprayed the room like shrapnel, but they were the soft kind, and didn't hurt much. If they had been my grandmother's sugar cookies, somebody might have been decapitated.

Most of our Cub Scout meetings from then on were pleasant but uneventful. We practiced our other knots—the hangman's had been banned—and worked on various projects thought up by Grover. The most interesting of these was the snowball catapult, constructed in the den mother's backyard out of a two-by-four, a couple of bicycle-tire inner tubes, and various odds and ends. It was powerful. Mrs. Slocum thought it was some sort of teeter-totter, until it fired a ten-pound snowball across three backyards and nearly took out old Mr. Fuller, who was carrying an armload of firewood at the time. He thought he had been narrowly missed by a meteorite, which was fortunate for us. If he'd had any previous experience with ten-pound snowballs, we might have been in a lot of trouble.

More often than not, we didn't have time to work up an interesting project, because Mrs. Slocum came down with a "sick headache" almost every week, and we had to adjourn the meeting early. I remember how disappointed we were when one of Mrs. Slocum's sick headaches forced us to abort Terry's test flight, after we had worked so hard to make him a parachute, in case he experienced technical problems during reentry.

Grover became increasingly bored, and I expected him to go AWOL at any time. Then one day in early spring, the scoutmaster of the local troop showed up at our meeting. Mr. Tiddle was a robust outdoorsman, shaped something like a barrel, but all bone and muscle. He frequently hiked his scouts into the ground and then ran up and down a mountain a couple of times just to work up a sweat, a feat about which he didn't mind boasting. He lifted weights and did calisthenics just for the fun of it, but the strangest thing was that every New Year's Day he would chop a big hole in the ice and plunge into the frigid water of Lake Blight. He claimed the icy plunge was wonderfully invigorating and recommended it highly to the local townsfolk. A few said they might give it a try, if their present supply of misery ran low and they had to restock.

"Boys," Mr. Tiddle boomed to us at our meeting, "I've got great news for you. A couple of the scouts from Troop Nine-oh-seven and I are going to take you Cubs on an overnight outing to Camp Muskrat this Saturday. How does that sound?"

We broke into cheers, with Grover cheering the loudest of all.

"You all show up at the school at eight o'clock Saturday, and we'll issue you sleeping bags and packs," Mr. Tiddle said. He then went on to tell us what clothes, grub, and gear to bring. "For supper, we'll treat you to a wiener roast."

"Yayyyyyyyyy!"

"It's about time we got to see some action," Grover said.

The next Saturday morning, about fifteen of us Cubs assembled at the grade school. Several station wagons were parked nearby. We assumed they were there to transport us to Camp Muskrat, located on a small lake five miles from town. Then we noticed that volunteered fathers were loading the station wagons with tents and other gear and supplies. We watched as the station wagons departed one by one, until none were left for us. We exchanged uneasy glances. Surely it was not intended that our short puny legs hike all the way to Camp Muskrat.

Mr. Tiddle and two Boy Scouts, all three in their

starched tan uniforms, strode briskly over to us. "Listen up, Cubs!" Mr. Tiddle bellowed in his most enthusiastic tone. "We have a real treat for you. Scouts Lucifer and Attila have volunteered to serve as your leaders on the campout, and they have come up with a marvelous idea. Instead of riding to Camp Muskrat, you get to practice your hiking skills all the way out to the camp. Let's have a big hand for these fine scouts."

Clap clap. We stared up at the towering scouts, both of whom smiled benevolently down on us. "I leave you in their care," Mr. Tiddle said. "See you all at Camp Muskrat." He got into his car and drove away.

The two scouts watched his car until it disappeared around a corner. When they turned back to us, we were shocked. They had grown fangs and claws and their eyes glowed red with fiery light! We could tell from their gleefully evil expressions this was an opportunity they had waited for all their lives.

"Hoist your packs and line up according to height, shrimps!" Attila bellowed at us in a pretty good imitation of Mr. Tiddle, only mean and threatening. "No talking! Move it! Move it!"

Startled, we hoisted our packs and scrambled into a ragged line, ranging from four-foot Peewee Thompson at one end to five-foot Leonard Brisco at the other. The packs had been intended for actual scouts and were too big for most of us. Peewee looked like a pack with legs.

"Hey, I just remembered," Porky Singleton cried out. "I'm supposed to go to the dentist today! See you guys later."

"I have to go to the bathroom," Danny Murphy yelled. "Be right back."

"Me too," shouted Tony Naccarado. "Be gone just a second."

"Shut up, shrimps!" snarled Lucifer. "Back in formation!" The would-be deserters shrank back into line.

"Left face!" screamed Lucifer.

"Forwarrrrd! March!" bellowed Attila. "Hut two three four, hut . . ."

Attila brought up the rear, apparently for the purpose of harrying the stragglers and shooting the wounded. We marched out of town and along the highway in a line that unkind observers described as looking like dusty blue gunk oozing from an invisible tube.

"How much farther is it?" croaked Peewee.

"Four miles to go!" shouted Lucifer, striding along. "Now close up that line! Hut two three four . . ."

The hot spots of blisters began to glow inside our tennis shoes. Pack straps gnawed at our shoulders.

"This ain't a hike," Grover muttered to me. "It's a death march!"

"Somebody is going to pay for this," I muttered back.

"You said it," Grover snarled, shooting Lucifer a wicked look. "Bring any rope?"

"Shut up, you two!" screamed Lucifer. "Hut two three . . ."

Hours later we limped into Camp Muskrat and dropped to the frozen, snow-blotched ground. Some of the packs looked as if they had finished the march on their own, but from beneath each crawled a wretched little blue-clad creature, one of whom was Peewee. "How much farther?" he gasped.

The fathers had set up the tents and then vanished with the blinding speed common to fathers volunteered for Cub Scout outings. Mr. Tiddle and the two scouts were now left alone with fifteen exhausted but surly Cubs, who sprawled in ominous silence, sullenly watching Attila, Lucifer, and Mr. Tiddle jog about gathering wood for the evening campfire. The scouts and scoutmaster joked and laughed as if they hadn't a care in the world. The air, however, was heavy with suspense, dark with foreboding.

I crawled over to the remains of Grover and Peewee. "Come up with anything for Lucifer and Attila yet?" I asked Grover.

"I'm thinking, I'm thinking," Grover said. "Everything I come up with is either too kind or too complicated. We need something simple but mean. I suppose we could steal their clothes so they would have to run around naked in the cold and maybe catch pneumonia and suffer horribly for a long time and then die terrible agonizing deaths. But I'd like to come up with something mean."

"I like it," Peewee said.

"Me too," I said. "But how do we get them out of their clothes?"

"That's the problem."

The sun sank behind Muskrat Mountain, and a breeze wafted in off Muskrat Lake, chilled by rafts of sludgy ice still drifting about the surface. We put on sweaters and even coats and gathered around the fire that Lucifer and Attila had built into a small inferno. This was more like it.

"Are we camping yet?" Peewee asked.

"I think so," I said.

Suddenly, Mr. Tiddle erupted from his tent with a towel thrown over his shoulder. "Any of you Cubs like to join me for a dip in the lake? What, no takers? Har har! Grow hair on your chests, boys, grow hair on your chests!"

"Grow hair all over me," Grover muttered. The other Cubs expressed the opinion that they had all the hair they needed or wanted.

"How about you scouts?" Mr. Tiddle boomed at Lucifer and Attila. "Like to refresh yourselves with a dip before supper? There's a nice sandy beach down the shore a ways, and we don't even have to chop through the ice. Just shove it out of the way."

Lucifer and Attila shuddered. "Why, we'd sure like to Mr. Tiddle. Sounds wonderful. But darn it all, we didn't bring our bathing trunks."

"Me neither," bellowed Mr. Tiddle. "Ever hear of skinny-dipping? C'mon, lads. Race you out to the floating dock!"

"Wow, okay then, Mr. Tiddle," whined Lucifer. "Attila and I'll be right there, as soon as we grab some towels. Hope we can find you in the dark." The two scouts slouched off.

We Cubs edged closer to the toasty campfire. "This is too good to be true," Grover said to me. At first I thought he was talking about the fire, but he wasn't.

"Be back in a bit," he said, and slipped off into the shadows.

Scarcely had Grover vanished when the plot thickened. The headlights of a car illuminated the Camp Muskrat parking area for a moment, and soon Mrs. Slocum and another lady came picking their way down a trail to the campfire.

"Good evening, Cubs!" cried our den mother. "You look like you're having a wonderful time. I'm so glad! I think you all know my good friend Mrs. Teasdale. We thought we would join you for the wiener roast. Brought you a treat—marshmallows!"

"Yayyyyyy!"

We pulled up a log for the ladies to sit on next to the fire. "My goodness, the mosquitoes are bad, and so early in the year, too," said Mrs. Teasdale. "Hope you all brought plenty of mosquito dope. Oh, I don't see Mr. Tiddle."

"He's out swimming," one of the cubs said.

"Oh, that man!" Mrs. Teasdale giggled. "He is simply too much."

Just then Grover emerged from the woods, slapping his way through a cloud of mosquitoes.

"Why, Grover, where have you been off to?" the den mother asked. "Not up to some mischief, are you?"

"Kind of personal, ma'am," Grover replied, trying his best to look embarrassed.

"Oh, I see. Excuse me, dear." The two ladies giggled in motherly fashion.

"Snatched only one set of clothes and a towel,"

Grover whispered to me. "Was all I could find in the dark. I could hear them splashing around not too far from shore and thought they might spot me. Slipped the clothes into their tent. But either Lucifer or Attila is going to be in for a big surprise!"

We sat around the fire telling ghost stories, but nothing compared to the horror that awaited us. Sooner than expected, Lucifer came rushing into the light of the fire.

"Wow," he said. "You guys are smarter than you look. That water is liquid ice. Just lucky I had the good sense to test it with my toe first. Toe's still numb. Man, if I'd jumped in that lake I'd have froze my—why, hello there, Mrs. Slocum, Mrs. Teasdale. Didn't know you were coming for a visit."

"Attila's the one," Grover whispered to me, snickering behind his hand. "This could be good."

A minute later, Attila bounded into camp—fully clothed! "Wheweee, that water's cold! Chickening out is the better part of valor, I always say. I don't know how Mr. Tiddle can stand it."

Grover stared grimly at Lucifer and Attila.

Minutes dragged by. We sang a camp song. Mrs. Slocum and Mrs. Teasdale told about when they were little girls and had picked huckleberries in the hills above Camp Muskrat. Terry started to tell another ghost story, and then . . .

The monster roared out of the darkness so suddenly that several Cubs almost inhaled flaming marshmallows. For a moment I thought it was a Sasquatch, but it turned out to be Mr. Tiddle. He was stark naked, except for a little cedar bough he had twisted off a tree as a concession to modesty and our tender sensibilities. He probably could have done without the cedar bough, because he wore a layer of mosquitoes thick enough to serve as a fur coat.

"So, the old steal-the-clothes trick!" Mr. Tiddle boomed.

"I thought this might happen," Grover whispered. "You can have my bike and baseball glove if you want them."

"Thanks, Grover," I said. "Hey, it's been fun knowing you."

Then a surprising thing happened. Mr. Tiddle grabbed Lucifer and Attila by the hair, one with each hand. "Ha! Just as I suspected—hair's not even wet! Well, I'll just have to see what I can do about that."

"Wait!" croaked Attila.

"It wasn't . . . !" blurted Lucifer.

"Oh, it wasn't, was it?" said Mr. Tiddle. "Well, we'll just check your tent and see if we don't find my clothes there."

"Good idea!" yelped Lucifer.

"You bet!" said Attila. "Check our tent!"

Mr. Tiddle dragged the two scouts over to check their tent.

"See," Lucifer said. "Your clothes aren't . . . NOOOOOO!"

"Aha!" cried Mr. Tiddle. "You two scalawags thought you could pull a fast one on me, did you?"

He snatched up each of the scouts by the back of the belt and charged off toward the lake, one in each meaty hand. The screams were among the best and most satisfying I've ever heard, starting low and quavering but then rising in pitch and volume while still conveying great feeling and intensity right up to the moment of total immersion. I thought I even heard one warbly scream from underwater, but it might have been a loon. We Cubs all agreed the performance was highly entertaining, spiritually enriching, and well worth a forced march.

Recovering his little cedar branch, Mr. Tiddle strolled back to the fire chortling. "Please excuse my nudity for a minute, boys. I just wanted to make a point about practical jokes—oh, nice to see you, Mrs. Slocum, Mrs. Teasdale. Didn't expect you ladies out this evening. The point I was making to the Cubs here is that people can play their little pranks, but in the end they have to pay the pipe— *Ladies?*" His lips froze in a grotesque smile over his big white teeth. He hunched over and tried to conceal himself behind the little bough. "Oh!"

I thought for a moment that Mr. Tiddle had blurted out a bad word, but then I realized a scoutmaster would never use a word like that. It was probably just the cry of some wild creature passing in the night.

Peewee said later that he thought it was all pretty funny, but that he couldn't help but feel sorry for Mr. Tiddle.

"I know what you mean," I said. "I sure would have felt embarrassed if I'd been standing there naked except for a little cedar bough and suddenly realized two ladies were sitting not ten feet away."

"Yeah," Peewee said. "Then, as if that wasn't bad enough, dumb ol' Terry accidentally flicks his flaming marshmallow onto the cedar bough. That ol' bough must have been dry as gunpowder, to flare up like that. Poor Mr. Tiddle."

"I think both Mrs. Slocum and Mrs. Teasdale handled it pretty well," I said. "It was nice how they pretended not to notice Mr. Tiddle because of concentrating so hard on twirling their sticks over the coals, just as if roasting wieners was the most important thing in the world to them."

"It would have been better if they hadn't let their wieners burn off and fall in the fire, though," Peewee said. "They didn't even seem to notice. Just sat there twirling them empty sticks round and round, and all the while Mr. Tiddle's roaring and darting about like a madman."

"Well, I guess that's camping," I said.

Grover never again showed up for a Cub Scout meeting. I guess he figured the campout at Muskrat Lake was the high point of scouting for him, and from then on it would be all downhill.

THE GROGAN LOOK

The Purdey Look

You will find at Purdey's a comprehensive range of waterproof waxed fabric clothing made to our own design, including jackets, trousers, shirts, and hats. We also stock ladies' loden cloaks, jackets, and culottes—in fact, everything that you need to keep warm and dry while out shooting. Shirts and ties and ladies' silk scarves, hand-knitted shooting stockings in a variety of colours, and knitted garters to complement them . . .

—FROM AN ADVERTISEMENT BY JAMES PURDEY AND SONS (ACCESSORIES) LIMITED, LONDON, ENGLAND, IN *COUNTRYSPORT*

You can imagine my consternation the other day when, upon pulling on my hand-knitted shooting stockings, I discovered that one of my hand-knitted shooting garters was missing.

"I say, old thing," I said to my wife, Bun, "have you by chance seen one of my hand-knitted shooting garters about the house?"

"I think the dog made off with it," she replied in a tone suggesting indifference.

"Why, the cheek of the beggar," I said. "He doesn't even wear stockings, the bloody fool. I dare say this is a sticky wicket. How can I possibly go shooting with the chaps if I have only one hand-knitted shooting garter? The lads will think I've gone balmy."

"You have gone balmy," Bun said. "And you'll drive me balmy, too, if you don't stop reading those British sporting magazines. And by the way, what was the idea of bragging to Harvey Puddwitt on the phone the other day that you own three Purdey shotguns? The only thing from Purdey's you own is a paperweight and a catalog featuring twenty-thousand-dollar shotguns."

"Mind, luv, I didn't say 'Purdey.' I said 'purty.' And I do have three of the purtiest shotguns Puddwitt is ever likely to see. Can I help it if he thought I said 'Purdey'? The bloke would jolly well have to be daft as a kipper to think that."

"Stop!" Bun cried. "You and your Brit sports magazines and your Purdey Look have got me tottering on the brink. I hope you're satisfied."

"Quite, old girl," I said. "And I would be even more satisfied if our smarmy bowser hadn't buggered off with my hand-knitted shooting garter."

"I hate to say this," Bun said, "but I found you much more sufferable when you affected the Grogan Look."

The Grogan Look. The very words froze me in the act of tucking my shooting tie into my waterproof waxed shooting jacket. It seemed almost impossible that I ever could have been so uncouth as to sport the Grogan Look. But, alas, it was all too true. One simply cannot escape his past, particularly if he has a blabbermouth spouse.

Henry P. Grogan, a stout, stubby little man with a bristly jaw and hard, greedy eyes, owned and single-handedly operated Grogan's War Surplus in my hometown. It was he alone who set the trend in sporting attire for our entire county. Had he ever bothered to advertise, the ad might have looked something like this:

The Grogan Look

You will find at Grogan's a comprehensive range of clothing made to our own design, including field jackets, combat boots, fatigues, web belts, wool trousers and shirts, ponchos, and parkas, most in trendy olive-drab color, and all guaranteed to be clothing. We also stock a variety of shooting jackets insulated with chicken down for cold-weather wear. Ammo belts, .45 automatic holsters, bayonets with sheaths, and steel helmets are available as accessories to complement your ensemble.

Grogan's was the haute couture of our hunting fra-
ternity. Everybody bought hunting clothes from Grogan, with the result that opening day of deer season
resembled a wildly disorganized invasion of the woods
by a division of U.S. infantry made up entirely of mis-
fits. Difficult as it is for a stylish sportsman like me to
admit, I too wore the Grogan Look. In place of the steel
helmet, I sported my exquisitely hand-battered red felt
hat, the band embellished with tail feather of pheasant.
This flourish of the gallant, however, in no way de-
tracted from the dominant effect, which was purely
Groganesque.

I bought my basic outfit when I was about fourteen. Grogan sold me a pair of olive-drab wool pants,
which struck me as a bit too large, but the proprietor
explained that the style that season was for the crotch
of the trousers to hang halfway to the knees. At that
age, I was already a slave to fashion and instantly
snapped up the pants. I knew at the very worst I would
grow into the trousers, provided I reached a height of
six-foot-six and a weight of 250 pounds. Furthermore,
there was plenty of room in the crotch to carry a
sweater or even a sack lunch. ("I've got an extra egg-
salad sandwich here, if you want it." "No thanks.") I
learned later that Grogan bought his pants by the bale
from the war department and apparently figured extra-
large could be cut down to fit any size.

"I'll have my tailor shorten those legs for you,"
he'd say, and carry them into the back room. "Take
about twelve inches off the legs, Pierre." *Whack! Whack!*
"Ah, thank you, Pierre!" Pierre himself was never seen

or heard, but for a Frenchman he was pretty handy with a machete.

When I cinched up the pants' size forty waist to fit my twenty-inch circumference, the excess yardage formed a series of accordionlike pleats around my middle and then billowed out toward my feet. The pleats, bulging fabric, short pant legs, and sagging crotch all combined to give me the appearance of being grossly deformed, but that was all right. Gross deformity defined the Grogan Look.

Henry P. also talked me into buying a pair of paratrooper jump boots. I have to admit they did look pretty nifty. "They'll keep your ankles from bending," Grogan told me. It was true. My ankles couldn't bend sideways or back and forth. As a result, I walked with a gait not unlike that of Frankenstein's monster. Small children fled in terror when I clumped past; dogs slunk away with tails between their legs and barks stuck in their throats. High fashion is not achieved without sacrifice.

Among other items of attire, Grogan sold me a wonderful chicken-down jacket that had been used by our troops in the Arctic, where I suspect they either froze or scratched themselves to death. The lumpiness of the jacket suggested some of the down was still attached to chickens. Nor was the jacket waterproof. Every time it rained, I went home smelling like a poultry farm.

One of the great things about my Grogan Look was the pockets. There were pockets forward and aft and on both sides, pockets on the legs and sleeves, pockets inside of pockets, big pockets, little pockets, square pockets and round pockets, dozens and dozens of pockets. The Grogan Look required you to cram every pocket full of something. You needed a map to find the pocket that contained whatever you were looking for, and even if you had such a map, it would be lost in one of the pockets. One of the worst things to lose in a pocket was a can of worms, although an egg-salad sandwich was a bad one, too. Either of these items lost in a pocket for a month or so became a social liability a good deal more serious than dandruff or bad breath.

The Grogan Look was chic for its time, and I'm not at all sure it didn't have certain advantages over the Purdey Look. For one thing, you didn't have to worry about your mutt running off with one of your hand-knitted shooting garters. My mates'll get a big kick out of that, the blighters, and just because they're all still traipsin' about in their Grogan Look.

THE SECRET OF
GOOSEY SMITH'S SUCCESS

It's always nice to run into an old childhood friend after forty years or so and discover that you had a hand in making him or her a great success. A while back I got a phone call from just such a person, G. Thomas Smith, president and chairman of the board of G. Thomas Smith International.

"Hey, old buddy," he said, "I hear you're going to be in town next week. How about us getting together for lunch at my club and doing a little reminiscing about old times?"

"Terrific!" I said. "What an absolutely splendid idea! I can't wait to see you. We had some great times, didn't we, pal? Gosh, I remember when we . . . But I'd better leave the reminiscing until we get together for lunch, old buddy of mine." After some more of the usual male-bonding banter, I hung up.

My wife, Bun, had been staring at me with a quizzical expression. "Who was that for heaven's sake?"

"Beats the heck out of me," I said. "But, hey, it's a free lunch. The guy says we chummed around together as kids, a G. Thomas Smith."

"It couldn't possibly be G. Thomas Smith of G. Thomas Smith International, could it?"

"That's the one. He must have me mixed up with somebody else. Still, he should be good for a pretty fantastic lunch, before he discovers his mistake. Wish I could remember a G. Thomas Smith from the old days, though. We had the usual collection of Smiths—Bobby Smith, Art Smith, Smith Smith, and a couple of others, but the only one I hung out with was weird ol' Goosey Smith. What a guy."

As I told Bun, Goosey never went anywhere without a couple of books and one of those pocket protectors crammed full of pens and pencils. I remember one time Retch Sweeney and I stopped by Goosey's house and he said he couldn't come out because he had to study. Later, Retch asked, "What'd he mean, study?" I said I'd heard of it but didn't realize people actually did it.

"Weird old Goosey," I said to Bun. "I wonder what ever happened to him."

"Don't you see?" Bun said. "The person you called 'Goosey' is now G. Thomas Smith of G. Thomas Smith International!"

"No! Impossible! But, by gosh, you may be right. It has to be Goosey!"

The following Wednesday I flew into the city

where Goosey lives. After meeting with a couple of editors in the morning, I took a cab to my old buddy's club. The club was even classier than I expected. It looked like a cathedral. I waited for Goosey in the vestibule, goggling at the massive oil paintings on the dark, paneled walls. Well-groomed chaps strolled about smoking big cigars and wearing suits that cost more than my house. The tables in the dining room bore creamy tablecloths and bouquets of flowers and linen napkins folded into little gleaming white tents. All the silverware seemed to match. I was mighty glad I'd had the foresight to change out of my Snoopy sweatshirt and into my sport coat with the yellow-and-green checks and my electric-blue tie. Otherwise, I'd have stood out like a sore thumb.

Presently, in strode a short, silvery haired man attired in a black cashmere overcoat, silky suit, conservative tie, and shoes so glossy they hurt my eyes. Everyone in the room shot to attention, and a couple of fawning attendants leaped to divest the gentleman of his overcoat. There was no question in my mind who it was.

"Goosey!" I shouted.

For a moment the gentleman looked startled, although not nearly as much as his fellow club members. Then he rushed over and wrung my hand. "Even after forty years, I'd recognize you anywhere, Pat," he cried. "Same rumpled look, same electric-blue tie!"

"Yeah," I said. "I was going to wear my other tie but thought you'd get a kick out of seeing Old Blue again. I'd better switch it off, though, before the batteries run down. Remember, I wore it at graduation from Delmore Blight High? You still got a pocket protector full of pens?"

"You bet," he said, pulling back his jacket. There it was, too, stuffed with gold pens.

"Hey, you look great, Goosey."

"Thanks. Uh, by the way, I'm not called Goosey anymore. I realize this may come as a surprise to you, but I was never particularly fond of that nickname."

"You weren't? I'll be darned. So what are you called now?"

"Mostly 'sir.' But you can call me Tom."

"You got it, Tom."

We went into the dining room, where I followed Tom's lead and ordered the luncheon special. I was pleased to see that it came with an hors d'oeuvre: a slice of liver about the size of a quarter and nine peas for decoration. I popped the hors d'oeuvre into my mouth and daintily licked my fingers while I checked out the other diners. They were all cutting tiny bites of liver with knife and fork. A couple of club members at the next table smiled grimly at me. Our snooty waiter came up and simpered, "Care for dessert now, sir?"

"What is it?" I replied. "Strawberry and cream? Thanks, pal, but I am stuffed. Woweee! Wait until the guys at Kelly's Bar and Grill hear about my lunch at Goosey Smith's club!"

Tom laughed. "Still the same old Pat, always joking around."

"Yeah," I said. "So tell me, Tom, what's the secret of your success? You were such a weird, fat little dork when we were kids, we never expected you would amount to much. I bet it was all that studying you did."

"The studying helped, of course, but the real secret of my success—and you're not going to believe this—was hanging around with Retch Sweeney and you."

"I don't believe it."

"Well, it's true. You two sharpened my instincts for survival in the world of business. Remember when we were about sixteen and you were fooling around with black powder?"

Of course I remembered. I went around for most of the year looking like an elongated cinder with glasses. Who could forget that? One day Goosey came over and asked how come I was wrapping friction tape on one end of a short, bent piece of water pipe.

"It's a pirate pistol, dummy," I said. "Anybody should be able to see that. The tape serves as both a grip and to hold the firing mechanism."

"Does it really shoot?"

"According to my calculations, it should," I said. "But I need someone to help me test-fire it."

"How about me?"

I studied Goosey for a moment. "Naw, I don't think you could handle it. This is very technical stuff."

"Sure, I can. Let me try. Please!"

"Absolutely not!"

"Please!"

"Okay."

I loaded the pistol, handed it to Goosey, and gave him instructions on the fairly complicated procedure for touching it off. "Aim for that bottle I set up on top of the fence post," I said. "I'll step off to the side here, so I can check on the ballistics better."

"You aren't leaving, are you?"

"Of course not. I'll be right over here, behind this cottonwood tree. Fire when ready."

Goosey fired. Right away I could tell the design required some modifications. For example, the muzzle velocity was much higher than it should have been. I estimated the muzzle was doing two hundred feet per second when it flew by my tree. As soon as my eardrums stopped vibrating, I walked over and pried what remained of the pistol out of Goosey's hand. He seemed to be in a mild state of shock, but otherwise none the worse for wear, except for some minor smoldering.

Tom and I had a good chuckle over the test-firing of the pistol. I took a sip from my water glass, even though the idiot waiter had somehow managed to drop a slice of lemon in it. I suppose I should have been thankful it wasn't something worse. "So firing that pistol taught you something that later helped you to succeed in business," I said.

"Yes, indeed," Tom said. "And that is: Never enter into a research and development project with a person who looks like a cinder. Otherwise, you're sure to get burned."

"Glad I was of some help."

"Then of course there was the raft you and Retch constructed when we were in fifth grade," Tom said, smiling.

I realized at once that he was referring to the time we had lost our control of the raft in some rapids. Refusing to panic, Retch had calmly grabbed Goosey, thrust him into the water at the stern of the raft, and used him as an outboard motor. Unable to swim a stroke, Goosey had clung to the raft and flailed his legs wildly, thereby generating enough propulsion to move the raft toward shore. By deftly twisting the lad's head this way and that, Retch was able to steer the raft to a safe landing spot, where he and I disembarked without getting so much as our shoes wet.

"A wonderful display of control and ingenuity," Tom said, dabbing his mouth with a napkin. "Those are essential attributes for success in business, not to mention a willingness to coldly sacrifice a weaker entity in pursuit of a goal. Say, do you by any chance recall that thing we did with the birch tree?"

One of our recreations as kids was climbing birch saplings until they bent over and slowly lowered us to the ground. There was an element of risk involved. Sometimes you misjudged the flexibility of the tree. You would climb up near the tip and then swing out into space, but the sapling would lower you only halfway to the ground, and you would be left dangling twenty or thirty feet in the air. The only thing that could save you was if one of your friends climbed the tree and contributed his weight to bending the tree the rest of the way to the ground. The friend could easily be persuaded to perform this service for nothing more than an expression of simple gratitude and the promise of an immediate transfer to him of all your worldly possessions.

Eventually, all the birch saplings within a mile radius of our homes were bent into the shape of a horse-shoe, and we had to run the risk of bending ever-stouter trees. One day I found myself dangling forty feet in the air from the tip of a deceptively unbendable birch. I frantically worked out the usual negotiations with Retch, who climbed up to the tip and swung out into a dangle alongside of me. The tree bent another ten feet, but we were still too high to drop safely to the ground. Finally, Goosey was pressed into service. The combined weight of the three of us bent the tree into a powerfully straining bow, leaving us with a drop of no more than ten feet. It was decided that all of us would have to let go of the tree tip simultaneously at the count of three. We chanted in unison: "One! Two!" Because neither Retch nor I trusted our associates in such matters, we both let go at the count of "Two." I can still hear Goosey:

"THREEEEEeeeeeeeeee-e-e-e—!"

It was his first flight. Nowadays, anyone in the air that long is served a snack and a soft drink. He said later he would have enjoyed flight more if he hadn't been so worried about the landing. The takeoff was sudden and violent. Years afterward, a woodcutter found the remains of a pocket protector nailed to a tamarack snag by two fountain pens and a pencil. It was a great mystery. Fortunately, Goosey was plucked out of the air by a thorn apple and suffered no injuries beyond moderate shredding.

"So, Tom," I said, "what did you learn from the birch-tree incident that helped you succeed in business?"

"Timing," he said. "In business, timing is every-thing. Never trust anyone when it comes to timing."

Tom and I chatted amiably a while longer. I confessed to him that Retch and I were financial fail-ures, still poor and struggling to make ends meet. Tom said he was glad to hear it, and thanked me for cheering him up.

As we were leaving the club, I invited Tom along on a two-week canoe trip with Retch and me, but he declined. Too bad. It probably would have been worth a couple of million to him.

# EASY ED

My wealthy friend Fenton Quagmire and I stopped by a boat display at an outdoor show a while back.

"How much for your jet boat there?" I asked the salesman.

"This is your lucky day, sir," he said, smiling. "I can let you have this baby at our special boat-show discount price of twenty-five thousand. And I'll toss in the trailer."

"Woweee! Toss in the trailer!" I cried. "Did you hear that, Quagmire? For twenty-five thousand, he'll toss in the trailer!"

"Yeah!" Fenton said. "Sounds like a great deal. But I'm a little short on cash. Do you by any chance have an extra five grand on you?"

Rich people really get on my nerves sometimes. "Gee, let me check," I said, digging into my jeans.

"Nope, I guess not. Wife must have gone through my pants pockets and taken all my change again."

"Quite all right," Fenton said. "The gentleman will probably take a check."

"Yes indeed," the salesman said, rubbing his palms together. "And how about you, sir? Anything I can sell you?"

"Not unless you have a plywood pram," I said.

"A plywood pram?" the salesman said, struggling to hold back a sneer. "I'm afraid not."

"How quaint!" Fenton said. "Why on earth would you want a plywood pram?"

"Nostalgia," I said. "I built one once—in high school shop class."

"Really, dear boy, you are full of surprises," Fenton said. "I had no idea you were handy with tools."

"Quite," I said.

"But why on earth do you harbor nostalgia for prams?"

"Oh, it's a long story."

"I was afraid of that."

"What happened was . . ."

Mr. Smathers, the shop teacher at Delmore Blight High School, had the reputation of being the meanest person on the faculty. He was a white-haired, gnomish little knot of a man with wild darting eyes and a facial twitch. His normal mode of communication consisted of a quavering, high-pitched shout with an occasional stutter worked in. It was said that in a quiet moment you could hear the tiny *fzzzt* sounds of his nerves fraying at both ends. That was why students in his shop classes long before our time had nicknamed him "Easy Ed."

On the first day of class, Easy Ed lined up all of us freshmen. Then he took a cigar box off a shelf and made each of us look at the contents—little shriveled-up pieces of meat and bone.

"Know what these are, people?" he shouted at us. "F-F-Fingers! These are f-f-fingers of f-f-former students who didn't pay attention to what they were doing while working around p-p-p-power t-t-tools! Next year at this time, your f-f-fingers could be in this box, too! Do I make myself clear?"

Personally, I thought it a rather strange hobby for a teacher, collecting fingers, but to each his own I always say. Odd as it was, I nevertheless tried to feign some interest in the collection, so as not to hurt Easy Ed's feelings. People can be sensitive about their hobbies.

Retch Sweeney raised his hand. Easy Ed nodded at him.

"Man, I can't wait to get at that table saw, Mr. Smathers. Can I be first?"

"No, me!" someone else shouted. Then others joined in. "Dibs on the lathe!" "I want the planer!" Guys started pushing each other and one kid fell against the band saw and ripped his shirt. Gordy, the class bully, experimented with clamping a kid's head in a vise. Shop class was going to be fun!

"Quiet!" Easy Ed shouted, his face convulsing in a massive twitch. "I have one more point to make and that is—TURN OFF THAT SAW, SWEENEY!—and that is, every year some loons sign up for shop with the notion they're going to build a boat. No boat building! Absolutely no boats! Delmore Blight High School has a firm policy against boat building in shop. The only projects you are allowed to work on this semester are bookcases, firewood boxes, and cedar chests. No boats!"

"There goes our twenty-one-foot sailboat," I said to Retch, who was testing the sharpness of the saw blade with his thumb.

"In that case," Retch said. "I guess there's only one thing to do."

"What's that?"

"Build a pram. Maybe we can rig a sail on it later."

"We can't build a pram," I said. "We have to build a stupid cedar chest or a bookcase or a firewood box."

"We'll build it in secret. Easy Ed will never know, at least until it's too late for him to do anything about it."

I was amazed that Retch could even think of such a thing. In all the time I'd known him, this was the only decent idea he'd ever had.

Retch found plans for the pram in a magazine. The plans looked simple enough, but then they always do. Our scheme was to cut all the parts first and then, in a single frenzied effort, assemble them into a pram before Easy Ed knew what was happening. We had to work fast, though, because all the lakes and streams would be frozen solid in a couple of months. Neither of us could bear the thought of having to wait until spring to try out our pram.

"We have to start working on the pram during lunch hours," Retch said. "Otherwise, we'll never get it finished in time."

"You're right," I said. "Besides, I find it hard to concentrate with all the screaming and yelling in shop class."

"Yeah," Retch said. "I don't know why Easy Ed screams and yells so much. Maybe he can't stand the sight of blood."

The next noon hour, Retch and I rushed to the door of the shop, but it was locked. Retch got out his jackknife, slipped it into the door crack, and forced back the bolt. We locked the door after ourselves, and turned to see Easy Ed glaring at us from his desk, a sack lunch in front of him. He was gnawing a fried chicken wing.

"What do you two want?" he growled, tossing the chicken-wing bones into the cigar box with his finger collection.

"Gee, Mr. Smathers," I said, startled, "we thought you'd be down in the boiler room sneaking a smoke with the other teachers."

"I intended to sneak it in here," Easy Ed said. "That's why the door was locked, so I wouldn't be setting a bad example for students."

"No problem," Retch said. "Just don't think of Pat and me as students."

"Actually, I never have," Easy Ed said, shaking out a cigarette. "So, to what do I owe the pleasure of this visit during my lunch break?"

"Oh, we're getting behind on our project," I said.

"We thought we'd work on it during the lunch hour, when we could have the power tools to ourselves."

"P-p-power t-t-tools," Easy Ed said, lighting another cigarette. "Oh, all right, go ahead. But watch your f-f-fingers!"

Later Retch asked me if I'd ever before seen someone smoke two cigarettes at once. I said no I hadn't, but I supposed that if you had to squeeze a whole day of smoking into a lunch hour, that was what you had to do.

"Another odd thing," Retch said. "You ever notice the only time Easy Ed stutters is when power tools and fingers are mentioned in the same breath?"

"Yeah," I said. "What do you suppose it means?"

Every noon hour from then on, Retch and I worked frantically crafting the parts for our pram. The day finally came when all the parts were finished. Already there were occasional snowfalls and some of the farm ponds were frozen over. Soon there would be no open water at all on which to test the pram.

"We got to start assembling today," Retch said as we rushed toward the shop one noon hour.

"Gee, I'm a little nervous," I said. "What do you think Easy Ed will do when he sees we've built a pram?"

"What can he do?" Retch said, chuckling. "Flunk us? You ever hear of anybody flunking shop?"

"Three-Fingers Malloy," I said. "He's the only one I can think of."

"Right."

Easy Ed had taken to sneaking his smokes in the boiler room, so we had the shop to ourselves at noon.

We pounded and screwed and glued madly for an hour and then dragged the partially completed pram over to a corner of the shop and stacked boards around it for concealment. A week later, we were putting the finishing touches on the pram. We had just stepped back to admire the secret fruit of our labor when suddenly the door opened and in walked Easy Ed. He strolled over and stood frowning down at our pram.

"So this is what you two have been up to!" he shouted.

"It's uh uh uh uh," Retch stammered.

"I can see what it is!" snapped Easy Ed. "A firewood box! I'm not blind, you know. But it is without a doubt the ugliest firewood box I've ever seen!"

Retch and I were crushed. "You think it looks like a firewood box?" I asked.

"Of course it does. But besides being ugly, it's way too big. I want this monstrosity out of my shop today. If the principal ever found out two of my boys turned out a firewood box that looked like this, he'd fire me on the spot. Get rid of it!"

Retch and I were now faced with the classic problem of all boat builders: how to move the boat once it's built.

"We don't have any way to move it!" Retch cried.

"Oh, for pity's sake," Easy Ed said. "It's got to be moved. Okay, I'll tell you what. Tomorrow's Saturday. You two oafs meet me here at nine and we'll load it in my pickup and haul it to the dump. And don't be late!"

The next morning we loaded the firewood box into the bed of Easy Ed's rusty old pickup. He was in a terrible mood, snapping and snarling at us as we climbed into the cab with him. Not only had we intruded on his Saturday, he growled, he was missing the Notre Dame football game, as though it was our fault his crummy pickup didn't have a radio in it. Presently he calmed down and sank into a sullen silence. He hunched over the steering wheel, squinting out through the cracks and grime of his windshield.

"You missed the turn to the dump, Mr. Smathers," Retch said.

"Shut up, Sweeney," Easy Ed said. "It's too far to the dump. We'll toss this ugly box someplace closer."

"Like where?" I said.

"I don't know," Easy Ed said. "I guess maybe we'll just drop it in the lake. Probably sink right to the bottom, so it won't be an eyesore."

Retch and I thought about this statement for a while. "Gosh, Mr. Smathers," Retch said, "maybe if the firewood box floats, Pat and I could find a couple of boards and paddle it around a bit."

"Well, I guess that'd be all right. I'll miss the game anyway, thanks to you two loons. If I recall correctly, there may be a couple of canoe paddles under that tarp in the back of the truck. But I wouldn't count on that firewood box floating for long."

An old codger strolling on the beach stopped to watch Retch and me paddling around at the edge of the lake.

"Strange-looking pram," he said to our shop teacher, who was hunched into his mackinaw and glowering at us. "You build it?"

"Nope. The boys built it in my shop class at the high school. But it's not a pram. It's a firewood box. Boat building isn't allowed in the shop class."

"Well I'll be danged! Sure looks like a pram. Seems to be leaking pretty bad, though."

"Most firewood boxes do."

"True. You're a shop teacher, huh? Sends shivers down my spine, just thinking about all them tender young fingers mixing with power tools. Get on your nerves much?"

"S-s-some."

"By the way, my name's Zack Simmons. You must be Mister . . . Mister . . ."

"Just call me Easy Ed."

YOU CAN SEE
BY MY OUTFIT

So you need to know how to prepare for your first outfitted hunt. Well, rest assured you have come to the right person for expert advice on the subject, no matter what you may have heard from certain blabbermouth outfitters of my acquaintance. Let's get started.

What about underwear? You may have noticed illustrations in sporting-goods catalogs showing four or five smiling guys standing around the hunting-lodge fireplace in nothing but their underwear. No doubt this caused you some concern, and rightly so. It certainly would me, if I didn't know that such scenes are unheard of in real hunting lodges. The appearance of your underwear is unimportant. Any old droopy pair of long johns will do.

Here is a tip: Instead of long johns, wear a pair of your wife's panty hose. The panty hose will help prevent saddle soreness, or, as I call it, horse burn. It is a good idea, however, not to wash out your panty hose in front of another hunter with whom you're alone in a spike camp. Few hunters have heard of wearing panty hose to prevent horse burn, and a spike camp is a poor place to try to explain it to them. Keep it a secret between you and your horse.

How much underwear should you take on a two-week hunt? One pair is sufficient. Hunters never change any of their clothes during a hunt, no matter how long they're out. If you are hunting in grizzly country, however, you may want to take a backup set of underwear, just in case. (Should you startle a sow griz with cubs, your first set of underwear may get badly shredded. That is the only reason I mention it.)

In regard to other clothes, take enough to fill out your duffel bag nicely. You won't actually wear any of these clothes, but they will give your duffel bag the proper shape. Because hunters never change their clothes or bathe during a hunt, I should mention the canaries. As you probably know, old-time miners used to carry a cage of canaries into the mines with them. If toxic gases were present, the canaries would alert the miners by toppling dead off their perches. For this same reason, many outfitters place cages of canaries in tents occupied by two or more hunters. Occasionally, an unscrupulous outfitter will sneak into the tent early in the morning and replace dead canaries with live ones, so the hunters never know they are being exposed to high levels of toxic fumes and don't report the outfitter to the Environmental Protection Agency. Just to be safe, you may wish to take your own canaries.

If you have never mounted anything higher than a tall bar stool, you may wonder if you should take riding lessons before setting forth on an outfitted hunt. The answer is no. The less you know about horses, the better. The only thing to remember is you're the one who's supposed to be on top. It is my opinion that if horses were meant as a mode of transportation, they would have come equipped with running boards, bucket seats, a steering wheel, and brakes—especially brakes. They have none of these. If you insist on practicing to ride a horse in the mountains, I suggest you get a hundred-gallon steel barrel and place a doily on top of it for a saddle. Build a fire in the barrel. When it is hot enough to fry an egg on, straddle the barrel and bounce up and down on it for three or four hours at a time. Every so often, have your wife sneak up behind you and try to knock you off the barrel with a branch or whack you across the leg with a club. After a few hours on the barrel, you will feel like howling out in anguish. On the actual hunt, however, howling in anguish only encourages the horse to invent more mischief. Therefore, you must learn to disguise the howl as a yodel, something like: "Eee-odellay-*AAAAIIIIEEE*-odelayeee." Practice at home. Sometimes it works, sometimes not. Actually, you might just as well save all this torture for the pack trip. Why go through it twice?

If this is your first outfitted hunt, and you have just bought a brand-new pair of cowboy boots, you may be tempted to beat up the boots so that they look well used. This can be dangerous to your health. The outfitter will look at your boots and then tell one of his wranglers, "Put Mr. Jones there on Nightmare and see if he can't get that horse tamed down a bit." Yeah, right. In truth, outfitters would never name a horse Nightmare. Their horses are all named Old Joe, Old Sam, Old Muff, Old Something. Horse names are interchangeable. It really doesn't matter what the horse is named, because horses are too dumb to know their names anyway. Wranglers use a generic name for all horses, as in "Whoa, you bleeping bleep of a bleep, whoa!"

If you are a sensible person and not hung up on a macho image of yourself, you may wish to inquire of the outfitter in advance whether he has a mule you can ride instead of a horse. A mule is a smart, level-headed, sure-footed mount. The outfitter will immediately be impressed by your good judgment. "Finally," he will say to himself, "I have got myself a sensible client. Here is a man who doesn't believe he will be transformed into Clint Eastwood by riding a horse. He doesn't care a hoot that it is always the comic character or a nun who rides the mule in Hollywood Westerns." That is exactly what the outfitter will say to himself. I, of course, always go with the horse. My Clint Eastwood squint just wouldn't have the same effect from the top of a mule.

You should always take a survival kit with you on outfitted hunts, because you never can tell when you might have to spend the night out alone. The kit should contain only the essentials for sustaining life: poncho, matches, salt, flour, dried fruit and soup, jerky, television set, knife, and compass. The compass is optional. All the typical compass does is point north, which is fine if you want to go north. If you can find a compass that points toward camp, buy it. A two-way radio might seem like a good idea, but it really isn't. The lost hunter radios the outfitter and says, "I'm lost, Ed." The outfitter replies, "Okay, where are you?"

In preparation for an outfitted hunt, you should target-practice with your rifle until you can group your shots into a circle the size of a dollar at three hundred yards. You should also practice swinging a baseball bat in order to improve your coordination and timing. In the actual hunting situation, you and your guide will climb two or three mountains looking for elk. Often you will crawl a half mile or so on your belly to get within range of a huge bull with the biggest rack the guide has ever seen in his life. You finally get in position for the shot. All your guide's skill and effort over the past two weeks have been directed toward putting you in this position. The whole hunt culminates at this moment. You miss the shot. The elk bounds away. Now you must react quickly. Drop your rifle and hit the guide with the baseball bat while he is still too stunned to grab you by the throat.

An outfitted hunt is a wonderful experience, and every hunter should strive to fit at least one into his lifetime of hunting. There simply is something heroic and satisfying about riding a horse high up into the mountains after big game. After a long day in the saddle last fall, I came riding Old Joe down a steep, twisting trail just as the sun was setting, my cowboy hat tilted low over my eyes, my Clint squint working nicely, and my echo bouncing off a distant ridge: "Eee-odellay-*AAAAIIIIEEE*-odelayee." It was nice.

FORGET DESIRE

Let me state right off that I am no athlete. I get shin-splints from a fast game of chess. My only form of exercise is climbing a high bar stool and bending an elbow. I once tried some yoga exercises, but when I did the headstand, everything went black, and I couldn't breathe. It was scary. Then I realized it was because my fat had rolled down over my head. Given this preamble, you surely will be surprised to learn that I was a first-string lineman on Sandpoint High School's 1951 championship football team.

Although I was as slow as an iron toad, I was also skinny and weak. Apparently these attributes in a football player impressed Coach Cotton Barlow a good deal, because he picked me for offensive guard. I weighed 150 pounds. The center, Chuck Balch, also weighed 150 pounds, as did the left guard, Allen Stuberude. We were the best personnel available to Barlow, the Girls Pep Squad being off limits. He really had no choice but to go with us, as he freely admitted to the townsfolk.

At the beginning of every football season, Barlow lectured us on the two main ingredients of a winning season: DESIRE and physical conditioning. "DESIRE! DESIRE! DESIRE!" he would shout at us. Remembering the plays was a good one, too, but DESIRE and conditioning were the keys to winning. Maybe the other teams were bigger and better than yours, but you could beat them if you had enough DESIRE to win, and if you could outlast them. DESIRE was the easy part. I had made a hobby of DESIRE, but the objects of it related only incidentally to football.

It was the physical conditioning that was terrible. Before every practice, Barlow ran us through a torture known as the "Burma Road." About twenty tackling dummies were arranged in a circle around the field, and we had to run around the circle alternating hip blocks and shoulder blocks into the dummies, until only two or three of us were left standing. It was more like the Bataan Death March than the Burma Road. If you were dumb enough to look down at the ground between dummies, you could make a pretty good guess about what had been served for hot lunch that day. The Burma Road was awful. Forget DESIRE. It was the Burma Road that won us football games.

Being the great coach that he was, Barlow relied not only on DESIRE and conditioning but also subterfuge. He disguised the puniness of the middle of his offensive line by buying us gigantic shoulder pads, which gave each of us the appearance of weighing at least twenty pounds more, not to mention the shape of an inverted equilateral triangle. Our shoulders were so broad, we had to turn sideways to get through the locker-room door. (Our team photograph shows us as tiny heads atop massive bodies.) Barlow's strategy may not have been directed so much at impressing the opposing linemen as it was at us. I for one could walk into the locker room feeling small, timid, and weak and walk out in my shoulder pads feeling big, mean, and powerful. My climbing into those shoulder pads was a lot like Clark Kent's stepping into a phone booth.

The first game was the big test. I can't remember our opponents and it would be too much exercise to look it up in the yearbook. But I do recall that we crushed the opposition. The middle three of the opposing defensive line outweighed us collectively by eight hundred pounds. They were huge. We demolished them anyway. It may have been because they were afraid to touch or be touched by such misshapen creatures, possibly androids Barlow had imported from another planet.

To make up for our lack of size, Chuck, Allen, and I invented a few techniques that haven't yet caught on among pro linemen. We would overlap our legs with each other, thereby linking ourselves together into a single unit. It worked well, and if the referees noticed, they didn't seem to mind.

I worked out some techniques of my own. Usually, I spent the game blocking some guy the size of a Hereford. I would shoot myself out straight and stiff into his midriff. He would then drive me back like a plow, my shoe cleats turning up furrows in the turf. By the time we reached the backfield, the ball carrier would be long gone.

We had a fast and flashy backfield. The person I usually blocked for was Leonard Plaster. Short and powerful, Leonard ran like a fireplug shot out of a cannon at the opposing line. Often, if no hole opened up, he blasted one out by himself. If I couldn't budge the defensive guard out of the hole, Leonard would run up my back, leap into the clear, and be gone. Sometimes he complained about the lack of traction, but in general he found my back a satisfactory launch pad.

The play I hated most, and Barlow's favorite, was one where I had to pull back out of the line, run around the right end, and block the linebacker. Leonard almost always beat me to the linebacker. This was infuriating, not to me particularly but to the coach. Not wishing to cause Barlow to suffer an attack of apoplexy right there on the sidelines, I decided I had to start getting to the linebacker before Leonard did, just for appearance's sake, if nothing else. I hit on a simple but ingenious solution. I would pull back out of the line and get a head start for the linebacker a count or two before the ball was hiked. It worked like a charm. I don't know why Barlow hadn't recommended this tactic to me himself. If the referees noticed, they didn't seem to mind.

I don't mean to imply that I was the only factor in our winning the championship. We had some great players on that 1951 Sandpoint Bulldogs team. One that comes to mind was an exceptionally bright sophomore by the name of Jerry Kramer, who went on to fame and fortune with the Green Bay Packers and as author of the book *Instant Replay*. Jerry helped quite a bit, too.

One by one, the teams of North Idaho fell before the juggernaut of the Sandpoint Bulldogs: Coeur d'Alene, St. Maries, Lewiston, Wallace, Kellogg, even Pullman and Central Valley, in Washington. Kellogg was by far the most fearsome. Their playing field had not a single blade of grass on it, only hard-packed, smelter-blighted bare dirt. One end zone was paved with a portion of old blacktopped highway. At that time, everyone in Kellogg stood over six-foot-four and weighed upwards of 250 pounds. Their cheerleaders could have bench-pressed the entire middle of our offensive line. The team itself was monstrous. We suspected that half of them had been miners for several years. Even more frightening than the team were the fans. We had to run our plays away from the sidelines, for fear our running backs might get tackled by someone out of the bleachers. Some of the substitutes they sent in were suspect. One of them wore a sport shirt and was smoking a cigar and carrying a can of beer. If the referees noticed, they didn't seem to mind. It was a tough game. Afterwards, we were hesitant to remove our uniforms, for fear of what might fall out—a kidney, a liver, a rack of ribs. But once again, we escaped with not only our lives but victory.

Finally, the only team that stood between us and an undefeated season was little old punky Bonners Ferry. It was hard, impossible actually, not to feel overconfident. Bonners hadn't won a game all year—starting to sound like an old B-movie script, isn't it?—and was the sorriest excuse for a football team we had laid eyes on. And we, the SHS Bulldogs, we had played the biggest and the best, and beaten them all.

We should have gotten some indication of what lay in store for us when the Bonners coach had his team do warm-up exercises in straitjackets and leg irons. These guys were criminally, homicidally insane. A long season of unrelenting defeat had driven them mad. By the last game of the season, they had become nothing more than crazed wild creatures of indeterminate species, although clearly carnivorous. Some of the larger specimens couldn't even be classed as bipeds.

We started the game armed with our usual DE-SIRE and superb conditioning. It soon became apparent we should have been armed with .45s. By the end of the first half, a pink mist saturated with particulates of bone, teeth, hide, and hair hung over the field. A dreadful truth began to dawn on us: puny, puky old Bonners Ferry was beating us! They were chewing up and spitting out our undefeated season right in front of us, and seemed pleased to do it. Even from the middle of the field we could hear Coach Barlow's arteries exploding like firecrackers. At one point, a Bonners tackle stood calmly on my face, one cleat up my nose, while he waited, arms outstretched, for Leonard to come through the hole that wasn't there. Sometime in the third quarter I was knocked cold, and glad of it. I lay on a stretcher on the sideline feigning continued unconsciousness, but Barlow apparently caught me peeping out from under an eyelid at the carnage on the field. He sent me back in. I felt as though he were sending me to my doom. My massive shoulder pads were now but an empty shell, and my only DESIRE was to get out of the game alive and in one piece. Actually, it was already too late for one piece.

Then, slowly, in the fourth quarter, the Bonners team began to falter. Their rage and frustration boiled dry. They shriveled and shrank before our eyes. They took on human features, brutish snouts and hooves changing into noses and feet. Soon, they became nothing more than a bedraggled bunch of high school boys in muddy football uniforms, so weary they had to take rest breaks going to and from the huddle. We had outlasted them! Their defensive line wilted pathetically before us, the wan and bloodied faces of the center, guards, and tackles filling with teary despair, as Bonners' one last chance for glory slipped irretrievably away. It was wonderful! In the remaining minutes, we scored effortlessly, even monotonously.

People little noted nor long remembered the heroic game Bonners played on that unhallowed ground, although it may well be that the ultimate judge of high school football games would have ruled that they deserved to win, and that our victory was but a hollow one. Tough tiddly!

THE GOOD SAMARITAN
STRIKES AGAIN

You probably heard about the fellow who rescued a person in distress and then vanished without even leaving his name. "Who was that heroic and modest guy?" bystanders asked.

It was me.

Returning from an ice-fishing trip a few years ago, I got caught in a blizzard at the top of a mountain pass. As I crept along through the blinding swirls of snow, a panel truck passed me. I decided to follow it, on the assumption the driver obviously knew where the road was. Presently, the driver smashed into a road divider, thereby ruining my perfectly good assumption, not to mention his truck. The truck bounced ten feet into the air and plopped back to the road.

This was the kind of emergency for which years of experience had prepared me. I stopped and calmly sized up the situation. This, by the way, is a good ap-

proach to emergencies, because it allows time for someone else to show up, someone who might be even more
of a take-charge guy than you are. But there wasn't
another vehicle in sight.

Despite an old war wound that causes my knees to
buckle during moments of crisis, I crossed the road and
peeked in a broken window of the crumpled and steaming vehicle. The dark interior of the car appeared unoccupied, but I spoke into it anyway: "How ya doin'?"
A stupid question is often the best kind in a crisis situation.

"Fine, buddy," a voice croaked. "I really like it
here in the glove compartment."

As my eyes adjusted to the dim light, I ascertained
that the victim wasn't actually in the glove compartment but pretty well compressed under the dashboard.
I knew better than to move an accident victim and
thereby cause him further injury. Still, I thought I
should do something. But what? The victim and I stared
silently at each other, he from under the dashboard and
I through the broken window. Maybe he would be
comforted by some light conversation, I thought.

"So, some storm we're having, huh?" I tried.

"I really don't feel up to light conversation at the
moment."

"Right. Okay, then, maybe I better have a look
under the hood," I said.

"Great," croaked the victim. "Go look under the
hood."

The hood was on the other side of the highway. I
went over and looked under it. Nothing. I can never

tell anything from looking under a hood anyway, but that's what my friends always say, "Let's have a look under the hood." It sounds good.

I walked back and looked in the engine compartment, then went back to the window. "Looks like you're going to need a little front-end work," I said.

"You're telling me," the victim croaked. "My truck's going to need some, too."

Suddenly, I thought of something actually to do. "Wait here," I said. "I'll be right back."

"No hurry," he croaked.

"You seem to be croaking," I said, thinking he might need a drink of water.

"You really think so?"

"Definitely. Maybe you're catching cold."

"Big deal," he said.

I went back to my car and returned with a water bottle and a blanket with which to cover the victim, but I couldn't budge the crumpled door. The only thing to do was to climb in through the window.

"I'm going to climb in through the window," I told the victim. "Don't be nervous."

"Why?" he asked, nervously, as if he expected me to rob him. "How come you're climbing in through the window?"

"I want to cover you up with a blanket so you don't catch cold," I said.

"Whatever," he said.

I brushed away the remaining shards of glass and slithered in through the window. It was so dark and cramped inside that I couldn't see what I was doing. I tried to feel along the victim's body so I could tuck the blanket in around him. My hand touched something wet and mushy. I gasped and jerked away.

"It's okay," the victim said, obviously attempting to comfort me. "It's really nothing."

"You call that nothing!" I said. "You're all wet and mushy!"

"Well, not exactly nothing. It's just a squished banana."

"Oh," I said. "Gave me a bit of a start."

"Yeah, me too, when I first noticed it. Actually, I wouldn't feel all that bad, if you didn't have your knee in my groin."

"Sorry," I said. "I'll just tuck this blanket around you until the ambulance comes. And now I'll pour a little water into your mouth."

"Aghhhh! That's my ear, you fool!"

"Strange place for an ear."

"Maybe you could just let me croak in peace, how about that?" He made a muffled sound.

"There, I've got you covered from the tips of your toes to the top of your head. That should keep you nice and cozy until the ambulance comes."

"Mph!"

"Hey, no problem."

All at once, cars and trucks were pulling up on all sides of us. Men began shouting at each other with the authoritative voices of people who are even better than I in an emergency: "I've got a fire extinguisher and a crowbar. Get a first-aid kit and some blankets. Somebody call the cops and an ambulance. Careful with that poor guy. His feet are sticking out the window."

Hands grabbed my legs and tugged me through the window. "Keep him straight, no bending, watch his arms and head," somebody said.

"Stop!" I cried. "I'm not hurt."

"Don't try to talk, pal. You're a little gushy in front."

"Banana. It's just squished banana!"

They laid me on a blanket. I struggled to get up but was pushed back down. "Don't move! You may have internal injuries."

"No, you don't understand, see, I was just driving my car and . . ."

"Could be some head injuries," somebody said. "His face is messed up pretty bad."

"My face is not messed up!" I shouted.

"Don't worry, pal! Plastic surgeons can fix you up better than new. Just take it easy. Don't try to talk. Here comes a cop and an ambulance."

Someone shouted over the wails of the ambulance and police car, "Anybody else in the wreck?"

"Naw, just a rumpled blanket and some junk under the dash. Here comes the wrecker."

Fortunately, the folks at the wrecking yard found the true victim under the dashboard and rushed him off to a hospital. He was released the next day, hardly the worse for wear. I heard he kept asking the identity of the Good Samaritan who covered him with a blanket, but no one knew. Once again the helpful stranger vanished without so much as leaving his name. I think it's better that way, I really do.

AH, SWEET POVERTY!

Scarcely had I settled into a lawn chair in the backyard, ignited my pipe, and poured myself a cool beverage than I detected an ominous sight. Two pink little paws appeared at the top edge of the six-foot-high board fence that surrounds the yard. Then came the irritating sound of little sneakers scrabbling for traction on the other side of the boards. Presently, an arm and a leg were thrown over the top edge of the fence. It was horrible. What made it horrible was that I knew the arm and leg were attached to Felton, the eight-year-old boy next door and the main reason for the fence in the first place. My wife, Bun, had refused to let me put coils of concertina wire along the top of the fence, and this was the result. Seconds later, Felton plopped into my yard.

"I see you hiding behind that rosebush!" he shouted gleefully.

"I was not hiding, Felton. I was down on my knees sniffing the soil to determine if the roses had enough fertilizer. So to what do I owe the pleasure of this visit?"

"I got bored and figured maybe you and I could do something together. I peeked through a knothole and saw you sitting out here all by yourself drinking and smoking. Don't you ever work?"

"Sitting out here all by myself drinking and smoking is my work, Felton, and I have to get right back to it. I hope you're not neglecting your TV watching. Got to get in your four hours a day, if you want to be average."

"TV is boring. You know what my problem is? I'm too rich. I wish I was poor like when you were a kid. Tell me again about you being poor. It must have been a lot of fun."

"Oh, it was, Felton. Every day we thanked the Good Lord for our poverty, we were having so much fun. The problem was we had more poverty than we knew what to do with. Several times I suggested to the Lord that he take some of ours and distribute it among our neighbors, so they could enjoy it, too. But poverty back then was sort of like zucchini squash; it was so abundant you couldn't give it away."

"What kind of toys did you have?" Felton asked.

"Well, let's see. I guess my favorite toy was dirt. I spent a lot of time playing in dirt. I built roads and tunnels and towns out of dirt. I'd populate the towns with little stick people and build stick forts around them, and sometimes I'd burn down the forts and massacre all the little stick people. That was a lot of fun."

"Gee, that sounds great!" Felton said. "I wish I had dirt."

"Yes, dirt was nice. Didn't require batteries, either. If they'd put dirt in Christmas catalogs, they'd probably sell tons of it."

"What other things did you do with dirt?"

"We threw it, for one thing. There was always a good supply of dirt clods around and you could throw the dirt clod at something and it would explode into dust just like a cannon shell or a hand grenade. Sometimes my friends and I would play war and throw the dirt clods at each other. If you got hit with a dirt clod, you were supposed to fall down, but if you smacked a kid in the body he would claim the direct hit by the cannon shell had only wounded him. If you hit a kid in the head with a dirt clod, though, he would fall down right away, without a lot of argument. So you always aimed for the head. Once Vern Schulze hit me right in the face with a clay clod, even though that weapon had been outlawed by the Geneva Convention. I still wish I had reported him for committing a war crime."

"Is that what happened to your face?"

"Nothing happened to my face, Felton. Now, do you want to be a wise elbow or do you want to hear about my being poor?"

"So what kind of shows did they have on TV back when you were poor?"

"There wasn't any TV back then. It hadn't been invented. We didn't know what we were missing, but later, when we found out what we had missed, we weren't disappointed. Instead of TV, we had water stains on the ceiling and my family would sit there in the evening staring up at the water stains. And somebody might say, 'Look, I see a dog chasing a cow up a flagpole in that one.' Everyone would laugh and say they saw it too, except for each of us maybe the dog was a tiger or Groucho Marx and the cow was a goose riding a bicycle. Everybody saw something a little different in the water stains. I remember once when my Uncle Fungus was still drinking, he shouted out that he saw a grasshopper dragging a bale of straw through a keyhole. Then we noticed he wasn't staring at a water stain but a keyhole. The only problem with water stains was that we, except for Uncle Fungus, of course, had to wait for the next rain for the channel to change."

"Gee," Felton said. "I wish we had water stains on our ceilings."

"Yeah," I said. "I wish you did too. Maybe someday they'll have a TV show starring water stains. I watched one the other day that came pretty close."

"So what other fun things did you have besides dirt and water stains?"

"Well, we had a crick," I said, pausing to relight my pipe. "It wasn't much fun being poor if you didn't have a crick around someplace."

"You mean a creek?"

"No, I mean a crick. A creek is what rich people had. Poor people had cricks. We didn't have any environmentalists back in those days, because we were too poor to have any environment, so the poor people dumped their old cars and trash and garbage and anything they didn't want anymore into the cricks. It was neat. When the spring runoff came, all that stuff was washed away, except maybe the old cars, and we poor people could start filling up the cricks again."

"What did you do with your crick besides dump stuff in it?" Felton asked.

"Oh, one thing we did was build boats to float down the crick during high water. Sometimes our boat turned out to be more submarine than boat, which was fun, too, if you knew how to hold your breath for a long time."

"Boy," Felton said, "if I had a crick, I'd build a boat and sail it off to Africa or some other interesting place."

"I'd help you build it," I said. "You'd like Africa."

"What else did you do with your crick?"

"Almost every day we went fishing in the crick and caught old boots and tires and occasionally even some fish. Most of the fish were small but sometimes we caught a seven- or eight-incher. One of the nice things about being poor was that when you came home with a mess of fish, your family went bonkers with excitement, because maybe they hadn't seen any protein-based food in about a month. It was wonderful, Felton."

"Gosh, I wish I had a crick to fish in every day and could bring home a mess of fish to my poor family," Felton said, staring off into space. "How come you called your fish a 'mess'?"

"I don't know. Maybe it was because they were often a mess, from being hauled around all day on a forked stick. We didn't have any catch-and-release back then, only catch-and-keep, and a limit was whatever you could catch plus one fish. The game department sets limits, of course, but they were so high almost no one ever caught a limit. Occasionally, you would hear someone say he had 'limited out,' but anyone who said that opened himself to stern criticism from his fellow anglers."

"Because he was a glutton?" Felton asked.

"No, because he was lying. Our game-department trout limit in those days was twenty-one fish, all over six inches. Limiting out was something fishermen dreamed about but never hoped to attain."

"So you never caught a limit?"

"In all truthfulness, Felton, I must confess that, yes, once I did."

One day Vern Schulze and I rode our bikes far up the crick, where nobody ever fished, because the stream there was but a trickle running through a tunnel of thick, high brush. We fought our way through the brush and dropped off the bank into the crick, which was scarcely deep enough to cover our tennis shoes. Our prospects did not look good. As we stood there in the green tunnel of brush, it became apparent that what we had heard about this section of the crick was indeed true. Glumly, Vern drifted a worm into a puddle about the size and depth of a cake pan. Scarcely had the worm taken a turn around the puddle than the earth opened up and attempted to suck Vern's line, rod, and Vern himself into its molten center. It was scary. I stepped back, so he couldn't grab my arm and drag me in with him. And then, miraculously, the Moby-Dick of brook trout burst up out of the puddle, shook its mighty head savagely, and then plunged back into the depths, which consisted of about four inches of water. Fortunately, Vern and I always fished with leaders strong enough to rope and hog-tie a steer, so it was but a few minutes before Vern hauled in with brute force the twenty-one-inch brookie. I stared down half in shock at the violently quivering body, the bulging eyes, the jaws opening and closing in great gulping gasps, never before having seen Vern reduced to this state. He sat in the water with his legs and hands desperately clamped around the struggling fish, as though it had come at him with a knife and had to get but one fin free to stab him to death. I finally recovered enough to cut a forked stick and thread the great fish onto it.

Only then was Vern able to speak. "Youph kazzoo mimph," he said, holding up the giant brookie in a manner calculated to invoke in me the greatest degree of envy.

Upon studying the streambed closer, we discovered that it ran back under clay banks, where the water was dark and deep. Beneath those clay banks lay a treasure trove of trout. Within minutes, I caught a brookie almost as big as Vern's, and then another and another. Vern was catching even more fish than I, because this is an arrangement we have, that he always catches more fish, while I catch smaller ones. By the end of the day, however, we both had our official limit, we had LIMITED OUT, and none of our catch was under a foot long. We released ten-inchers, believing them to be the puniest fish we had ever seen, fish that the day before would have broken our hearts with sheer joy. We complimented each other on our sportsmanship, as though it had been our lifelong habit, the releasing of fish.

In the dying of the light, we rode ten miles home, the trout-laden forked sticks lashed to our handlebars. Actually, it was only five miles to our homes, but we took the long route, past the houses of our friends and around town, and people would call out, "Where'd you catch 'em?" not expecting us to tell the truth, but we shouted back, "In the crick!" and they would say, "Sure. Right. But where did you really catch 'em?" Oh, it was glorious, absolutely glorious, and we still hadn't taken the fish home, where we knew our families would go berserk with ecstasy. And they did go berserk. It was wonderfully satisfying.

That was the finest fishing day of my life. Years later I would catch salmon the size of Buicks, but they never gave me the same charge as those clay-bank brookies. "Your father caught a salmon the size of a Buick," my wife—stifling a yawn—would tell the children. "Oh great," the kids would say, rolling their eyes toward the ceiling. "Can we order in pizza?" Not being poor takes some of the satisfaction out of fishing. That's probably one of the reasons there's so much catch-and-release nowadays.

"Gee," Felton said sadly. "I'm afraid I'll never get a chance to be poor. My dad makes too much money. I guess he just doesn't know any better. Well, I'd better go watch TV. I've still got a couple hours to do." He climbed back over the fence.

Much to my surprise, I felt sorry for the little fellow and thought I should really do something for him. Maybe for Christmas I'd give him a nice big bag of dirt and some sticks. It seemed the least I could do, particularly since I myself planned to ask Santa for some concertina wire.

MY UNSOLVED MYSTERY

One of my favorite television shows is "Unsolved Mysteries," possibly because I have so many unsolved mysteries myself. Take the mystery of "The Ducks in the Fireplace," for instance.

A couple of years ago, my wife, Bun, and I went up to our river cabin for a weekend. The day was a little chilly, so I decided to build a fire. I opened the screen on the fireplace and there was a dead duck, a mallard hen, reposing on the grate.

"Hey, there's a duck in the fireplace," I told Bun.

She approached cautiously. "This better not be one of your stupid jokes. My gosh, there really is a duck in the fireplace. Are you sure it's dead?"

"No, ducks always sleep on their backs with their feet sticking up. Of course it's dead."

"Don't pull your woodsy lore on me," Bun

snapped. "If a duck is dumb enough to fly down a chimney, it's dumb enough to sleep on its back."

Therein lay the mystery, of course. Ducks aren't dumb enough to fly down chimneys. I tried to imagine the duck perching on the chimney, losing its balance, and falling in. It was pretty hard to imagine. Mallard ducks usually don't perch on anything higher than a floating log, let alone chimneys.

"How about this," Bun said. "The duck is flying over the house and has a fatal heart attack and drops right down the chimney."

"Ducks don't have heart attacks," I explained.

"Oh, yeah, you're so smart, what do they have then?"

"I'll tell you what they have. They have coyotes and weasels and foxes to do them in."

"So you're saying a coyote was flying over the house and dropped the duck down our chimney, is that it?"

"No, that's not it! I'm saying . . . well, all right, I suppose it is possible the duck had a heart attack just as it was passing over our house and its trajectory was such that it went down the hole in the chimney. In fact I'm sure that was it! Satisfied?"

"She probably had a heart attack because of all the stress of having to put up with a cranky old duck husband, that's what I think," Bun said. "Now go give her a proper burial. She at least deserves that, after all her years of slaving over a—"

"All right, all right." I was about to add "Spare me the lecture on duck feminism," but thought better of it. I took out the duck and chucked it into the burn barrel, first scanning the woods for feminists. You never know.

A couple of weeks ago, Bun and I drove up to the cabin for a few days of fishing. As she was walking by the fireplace, Bun noticed ashes all over the floor.

"Look at those ashes!" she shouted. "It's just like you and your old buddy Retch Sweeney to leave a mess like this!"

I stared at the ashes. "We're innocent," I said, tidily knocking out my pipe in a flowerpot. "We'd never leave ashes all over the floor like that. What kind of slobs do you think we are?"

"Is that multiple choice or essay? Oh, for heaven's sake, go get the vacuum so I can clean up these ashes."

After Bun had vacuumed the ashes, we went out on the dock and caught a few perch for supper. I offered to flip a coin to see who cleaned the fish, but Bun was still miffed about the ashes on the floor and refused me even a sporting chance. She headed into the house to make a salad, while I dumped the perch on my fish-cleaning table. Before I had cleaned a single fish, Bun bounded out into the yard.

"What in the world have you been up to now?" she shouted.

I really hate vague questions like that. "Give me a category," I said.

" 'Slobs,' " she replied. "There are ashes all over the floor again, just after I cleaned them up!"

"You're my alibi," I said. "You've been with me the whole time. You think I have some kind of occult power that enables me to blow ashes all over the floor while I'm fishing off the dock?"

I went in to investigate. Sure enough: ashes all over the floor. I opened the glass screen on the fireplace. And there was another duck! A live duck!

The duck was wedged between the wall of the fireplace and the grate. It beat its wings and sent a cloud of ash over my head. Coughing, I stepped back and closed the screen, which obviously didn't keep the ashes from billowing onto the floor.

"What is it?" Bun asked nervously, her hands trembling about her mouth. I've noticed that every time we encounter one of these strange occurrences, Bun gets a look in her eyes similar to that of a sprinter tensely poised on the starting blocks. She projects a strong sense of "about to take off."

"Just the usual duck in the fireplace," I said, wiping ash out of my eyes. "This one's alive, though."

"I can't believe it!" Bun gasped. "How in the world could another duck get in our fireplace?"

"Couldn't have been a fatal heart attack this time," I said, scratching my head. "Maybe a bad case of indigestion, but not a heart attack."

"Well, don't just stand there! Get the poor thing out!"

I opened the screen and reached in to rescue the duck, who responded by flailing its wings and filling my eyes and lungs with ash, not to mention clamping its bill onto the tips of my fingers. Blinded and choking on ash, I danced around trying to shake the enraged duck loose.

"Don't hurt it!" Bun screamed. "Don't hurt it!"

Over half a century of poking around the woods and mountains, I have rescued several dozen wild creatures from life-threatening situations. Almost none ever expressed an iota of gratitude. Instead, they have attempted to bite me, peck me, claw me, scratch me, gore me, even as I rendered them the service. The only one to repay the favor of my rescuing it was a skunk, when I was eight years old, and it spent all of its resources to purchase my freedom from school for a whole week. In my experience, however, that skunk was unique among wild creatures for its kindness and generosity.

Now I was once again involved in an act of rescue, this time of an unappreciative duck, which I finally managed to subdue. I carried it outside, where Bun hosed the two of us off with a stream of icy well water, apparently forgetting that I had access to a hot shower. De-ashed, the duck turned out to be another mallard hen.

"Maybe we should take her in to the vet and get her checked out," Bun said.

"To a psychiatrist maybe," I replied, examining the flattened tips of my fingers. "But I can tell you with absolute certainty that I'm not taking a duck to a vet. And that's final!"

I carried the duck down to the river and tossed her into the air. Her wings and quacker still worked fine, much to my relief, because it's a thirty-mile drive to the nearest vet. She had her throttle wide open by the time she cleared my hands and zoomed off like a duck out of a fireplace. The last I saw of her she was rounding a distant bend in the river. Good riddance, too.

The mystery remains unsolved. How did not one but two ducks get into my fireplace? Or rather, why? Obviously, they had to come down the chimney. Have the ducks cooked up a plot against me merely because I have cooked up a few ducks?

The only theory I have, excluding the occult, is that an eagle or hawk snatches up a duck and then lands on my chimney to enjoy its meal. As soon as the claws relax, the duck zips down the hole in chimney. The eagle or hawk looks down at its claws and thinks, Am I losing my mind? I could have sworn I just caught a duck!

Here's a word of advice for anyone who finds a duck in his or her fireplace: Don't mention it to anyone.

Innocently, I told my friend Dave Lisaius that I'd found a dead duck in my fireplace. He looked at me with that odd, startled expression he gets when I report one of my strange occurrences to him. Then he doubled over and started emitting high-pitched squeals that I assumed were somehow expressions of mirth. Dave is strange. Once on a hunting trip, we were sitting out a three-day storm in my pickup camper, and I casually mentioned to him that I had fallen out of a moving bus when I was five years old and landed on my head. Dave laughed so hard he almost fell out of the over-cab bunk, which would have served him right.

"What's so funny?" I asked him.

"It explains so much!" he cried, wiping his eyes.

Really, I don't know why I hang out with Dave, the guy is so weird.

I had forgotten about Dave's reaction to my report of the first duck in my fireplace. Otherwise, I certainly would never have mentioned the second duck to him.

"What? Another one?" he shrieked. "It can't be true! You're just telling me this so I'll die laughing! You're trying to kill me! Stop!"

Aha! I thought. The perfect crime! "Yes, another duck in my fireplace," I shouted at him. "This one alive. It nearly blinded me by beating ash into my eyes." Dave was down on his knees now, gasping, holding up his hands, pleading with me to stop. I decided to finish him off.

"Furthermore, it bit me on the tips of my fingers. Very painful, a duck bite."

"B-b-bit h-his f-f-fingers!" Dave groaned in agony.

Unfortunately, Dave survived to spread the story of my two ducks around town. Every time I stop by Kelly's Bar & Grill some joker asks if I've found any more ducks in my fireplace, and all the Kelly Irregulars stand around with these great big stupid grins on their faces.

Or maybe I go into Gert's Gas 'N' Grub for lunch, and Gert comes up with her little pad and asks, "What's it going to be, ducky?" Always gets a big laugh.

Or I'm at home and my phone rings. "Hello, Pat? This is Robert Stack, host of 'Unsolved Mysteries.' I have a few questions to ask you about the ducks in your fireplace. First, have you noticed any spaceships hovering over your house recently or . . . ?"

I know, of course, that it's not really Robert Stack. For one thing, Mr. Stack isn't the sort of person to burst into hysterical giggles when he says the word *ducks*.

"Very funny," I say and hang up. You'd think a wife would have better things to do than make crank calls.

BRING ME ONE OSCAR, HOLD THE SARCASM

This was my big chance. Ever since second grade, I knew I had acting talent. Miss Jones, the teacher, had selected me from her twenty-odd pupils to be the Postmaster at the Second Grade Valentine's Day extravaganza. Usually, Miss Jones bestowed such honors on one of her seven or eight pupils who weren't odd, but this time she went with me, one of the odder of the odd. All my classmates were jealous, of course, particularly after they witnessed my wonderful performance. If they gave Oscars for Best Second Grade Valentine's Day Postmaster, I surely would have been nominated.

Then, as happens with so many actors, my career went into a decline. It wasn't until I was a junior in high school that I landed another part. True, I had only one bit of dialogue in the Spanish Club play, but I delivered it with such feeling that it stole the show. Even now I recall my speech in its entirety: *"Olé!"*

My acting career still failed to take off. Thirty-odd years passed. Five or six of the years weren't particularly odd, but most of them were. That, I suppose, is the fate of an odd person. But suddenly one day out of the blue I received a call from Larry Schoenborn, producer of the nationally syndicated television show "Fishing the West." Larry apologized for calling out of the blue rather than on the telephone. It had given me quite a start. At first I thought it might be God. (When God calls me, it usually isn't with good news.)

"Pat," Larry said, "I want you to star on my show, 'Fishing the West.' "

"Wow, that's great!" I responded. No doubt someone had told Larry about my Postmaster performance. "When does the shooting start?"

"The first of August."

The first of August! That didn't leave me any time to learn my lines or get in shape. I hadn't even begun to take off the weight I'd put on over the holidays—the holidays of 1972. Still, a little extra weight didn't seem to affect the acting careers of Orson Welles or Raymond Burr.

"When do I get to see the script?" I asked.

"There's no script," Larry said. "We make it up as we go along. We just try to act normal."

"Act normal," I said. That could be tough. I hadn't acted normal in fifty years, but I wasn't about to tell Larry. This, after all, was my big break.

"One more thing," Larry said, "I want you to pick a lake for us to do the show on, one of your regular fishing haunts."

I suggested Lake Pend Oreille, which I live on, but Larry said he had already done a show there. I next suggested my other favorite fishing lake, Lake Koocanusa, in Montana. I have fished all over the world, and Lake Koocanusa, with the exception of Sand Creek, is the only body of water on which I've always limited out. That's how good the fishing is. The river that runs out of the lake, the Kootenai River, is also one of the great fishing streams of America, but almost nobody knows about it. I would keep that fact a secret, except it is too far away from everywhere for folks to get to. Sometimes there is a crowd of up to six people fishing it, but usually I have the river to myself. One reason I have the river to myself is that most of the locals know that anytime I'm in the vicinity, the fish instantly go into a comatose state, sink to the bottom, and don't revive until three days after I'm gone. The locals tell visiting anglers, "You should have been here before McManus showed up. The fishing was fantastic."

Now, it's true I'm often skunked on the river, but, as I say, never on the lake. The lake is simply too large for my anti-magnetic fish-repulsion field to take effect. That's my theory anyway. And it's chock-full of kokanee, which is the fish Larry had indicated he wanted to fish for. What unnerved me, however, was that never before had I starred in a TV show on the lake. It would be my luck that we wouldn't catch a single fish during the shooting of the show! Beads of nerve-induced perspiration popped out on my forehead at the very thought. For the first time in the history of "Fishing the West," not a single fish would be caught. And I would be the obvious culprit, exposed to ridicule in front of millions of TV viewers!

Just to be on the safe side, I called Neven Zugg, owner of the only resort on the lake, Koocanusa Resort. "How's the fishing?" I asked Neven.

"Wonderful! Fantastic!" Neven said. "Who is this?"

"Pat."

"Oh. In that case, the fishing isn't that great this summer. The kokanee are mostly small, only about ten and twelve inches. We're at the bottom of the cycle. By next year the lake will be loaded with sixteen-inchers. The fishing will be wonderful. Fantastic!"

"No good," I said. "I'm starring in a 'Fishing the West' show up there in a couple of weeks."

"No!" cried Neven.

"Yes," I said. "I guess we'll just have to be satisfied with a show about the smallest fish ever caught on 'Fishing the West.'"

"It's not the fish I'm worried about! It's you! The TV viewers will think there's hardly a fish in the lake! I'll be ruined!"

"Don't I always catch my limit?"

"Yes, but your limit is only two! Everybody else's is twenty-five!"

"True," I said. "But I don't want you blabbing to the TV people about the size of my limit."

In preparation for my performance, I studied some of the fishing shows on TV to pick up the various techniques. One of the things I learned was that these shows have their own special terminology:

STATEMENT: "Wow, look at that scenery!"
MEANING: "We're not catching any fish."
STATEMENT: "Boy, I just enjoy being out here."
MEANING: "We're not catching any fish."
STATEMENT: "Wow, that's a pretty fish!"
MEANING: "We caught a small fish."
STATEMENT: "Wow, look at the size of that baby!"
MEANING: "We caught a fish slightly bigger than small."
STATEMENT: "Hey, look, a bald eagle [loon, sparrow, deer, muskrat, etc.]!"
MEANING: "We're still not catching any fish."

Bright and early on the day of the shooting, I met Larry and his video crew at the Koocanusa Resort. In addition to Larry, the host of the show, the crew consisted of Larry's wife, Ethel, and two cameramen, Gene Hiring and Willie Brosseau. They had about a million dollars' worth of television equipment with them. For some reason, an image leaped into my mind of all that equipment slowly settling toward the bottom of Lake Koocanusa. At least that's what happened the last time I was on water with television equipment. I thought it best not to mention this slight mishap to Larry.

Ed Zugg, father of Neven, volunteered to drive the camera boat. Ed's one of those irritating guys who catch fish when nobody else does, thereby canceling out the excuse "they're just not biting today." I was glad Ed would be driving a boat and not fishing.

"I understand from Pat he has limited out every time he's fished this lake," Larry said to Ed.

Ed laughed. "Yeah, that's true. But his limit's only . . ."

Neven poked his dad in the ribs and shook his head.

"Yeah, that's true," Ed said.

We shoved off and ran a few miles up the lake to one of my favorite fishing spots. I explained my techniques for fishing the lake and recommended some lures as Willie and Gene shot away. The rest of the day went smoothly, except for the big rock. I don't know why I can't remember that rock, after all the times I've hit it. I'm sure the screams and various spontaneous outbursts of colorful language can be edited out and won't mar the finished show. Fortunately, the water wasn't all that cold, and I actually enjoyed getting a little practice on my backstroke.

The fishing turned out to be about normal for me. I limited. And I did a fine job on the dialogue.

"Wow, look at that scenery!" I exclaimed with fervor. "Wow, look, a bald eagle! Wow, that's a pretty fish! You know, I just enjoy being out here!"

In all modesty, I must admit that my performance may even have surpassed my acting in *Valentine's Day Postmaster*. I'd better get in as much fishing as I can before the show airs. After that, I'll probably be too busy doing lunch and taking meetings with Hollywood producers.

THE FLASHLIGHT MAN

Of all my wonderful summers, I'd have to nominate the summer of 1947 for Best All-Around Summer. Besides its other fine features, that was the summer of the Flashlight Man.

Several girls reported that while they were walking home from the evening movie, a man wearing only swimming trunks had leaped out of the bushes and shined a flashlight on himself. The weird thing was that he had painted himself all over with a bunch of different colors. Maybe he was the first person to come up with the idea of body painting, and was just trying it out for effect. In any case, it got a rise out of the girls, about two feet by most accounts, and they never touched down until they reached home.

It seemed like a fun thing to do, and my friend Retch Sweeney and I thought we might give it a try, too, just for entertainment. But then we heard the police were looking for the Flashlight Man, and decided that maybe the idea wasn't so good after all. It had never occurred to us that scaring girls was a crime. At age twelve, we more or less thought of it as a minor-league sport.

Our summer dragged along at a pleasant, leisurely pace, punctuated by frequent fishing trips into the mountains and an occasional camping trip. Retch and I slept out almost every night on his lawn, conditioning ourselves to the dark, philosophizing about life, slapping mosquitoes in midair to sharpen our reflexes, and watching the nighthawks flash through the glow of the corner streetlight like erratic meteors. Several nights we went prowling on the warm dark leafy streets of town, hoping to capture the Flashlight Man and become heroes. Although reports continued to come in of his appearances, we never spotted him. The summer of '47 continued to drift pleasantly along.

One day Retch came over to my house with interesting news. "Hey, guess what. My old man's gonna paint his gazebo."

"Good gosh!" I exclaimed, not a little astonished. I knew Mr. Sweeney was strange, but this was a bit much. "What on earth does he want to do that for?"

"It's starting to peel and flake."

"Geez, that's awful!"

"You want to come watch him paint it?"

"Naw, I don't think so."

"C'mon, it'll be fun. He's rented an air compressor and a spray gun."

"A spray gun? What exactly is a gazebo, anyway, Retch?"

"Don't you know nothin'? It's that funny little round building in the park down the street from our place. Popper built it for the park department years ago. It's got all that latticework on it and no walls, just some posts holding up a roof."

"Oh, that! Sure, I'll come watch. Sounds like fun."

We got on our bikes and pedaled off to the park. We hadn't missed any of the fun, because Mr. Sweeney hadn't started painting the gazebo yet. He was sitting on a park bench, glumly drinking a beer. He was dressed in his painting coveralls, even though the temperature was at least ninety degrees in the shade. Streams of sweat trickled down his face. He peered around his upturned beer bottle at Retch and me, humorously concealing his pleasure at our arrival by rolling his eyes upwards in an expression of feigned annoyance.

"Hi, Popper," Retch said. "How come you're sitting out here guzzling beer when you're supposed to be working?"

"If it's any of your business, Retch, I hate painting. It may take me three beers just to get started. I trust you two are just passing through."

"Naw, we come to watch you paint your gazebo."

"Oh, great!" Mr. Sweeney said, which surprised me, because he usually didn't like Retch and me hanging around while he worked.

"Hot as it is, you're going to cook in those overalls," Retch said.

"I'm already half cooked," Mr. Sweeney said. "But I don't want to get paint all over any other clothes."

"You know what I'd do if I was you?" Retch said.

"What, pray tell."

"I'd put on those old bathing trunks of yours. After you're done painting your gazebo, you could just go for a swim in the lake and wash off."

"Hey, that's not a bad idea," Mr. Sweeney said. "Maybe the old Sweeney genes are starting to kick in."

"Thanks," Retch said. "But forget the jeans. Your old swimming trunks would be better."

"So I was wrong about the genes," Mr. Sweeney said. "I'll just borrow your bike and ride home and change into those old trunks of mine." He mounted Retch's bike and pedaled off in comical fashion, his long legs canted out and his knees pumping up almost to his ears, because the bike was much too small for him. It was too small even for Retch. We were still laughing about the amusing spectacle, when Mr. Sweeney came pedaling back, wearing only his old swimming trunks, which were also too small for him. The sight of Mr. Sweeney riding the too-small bicycle and wearing the too-small swimming trunks renewed our attack of mirth.

"What's so dang funny?" Mr. Sweeney said, glaring at us.

"Nothing, Popper," Retch wheezed. "We was, uh, just talking about, uh, a funny thing that happened last year in school."

Mr. Sweeney hooked up the spray gun to the air compressor and started painting the gazebo. It was interesting at first but soon became monotonous. Retch and I wandered off to see if we could find something a bit more entertaining in the park. We tried out the swings in the play area, and Retch pumped his up so high, the swing didn't swing back but dropped straight down with such force it compacted Retch into a condensed version of himself, like a cartoon character that's had an anvil dropped on it. "Stupid swing!" Retch said, stretching out into his original height. "Almost killed me. You wouldn't think they'd have dangerous things like that in a park." We moseyed off in search of less dangerous entertainment.

Toward evening, a breeze came up, and we drifted back toward the gazebo, thinking that maybe a little wind might make the spray painting of the gazebo more interesting. It had, indeed. Only about half the paint was going on the gazebo. Most of the other half was billowing out around Mr. Sweeney. He was covered with white paint from head to foot.

"Holy cow, Popper!" Retch cried. "You're covered with paint. And look what you've done to my bike! You've painted it white, too!"

Mr. Sweeney's red fierce eyes glared out of the surrounding whiteness.

"But I kinda like it," Retch added.

"Good!" Mr. Sweeney said. "Now, all I have to do is touch up some of the inside trim with a little red and green paint and I'll be done. Woweee! I can't wait to dive into the lake."

Retch and I watched his father paint the overhead trim with a brush. Some of the red and green paint dribbled down onto his coating of white paint. The effect was perhaps not unattractive, if you were into abstract art, which neither Retch nor I was.

Mr. Sweeney stepped back to admire his work. It looked pretty good, at least in the gathering dark. "Not bad, if I do say so myself," he said. "Now you boys take the spray gun and compressor and other tools home, while I ride Retch's bike down to the lake and wash off this paint." We loaded the compressor and other tools into Retch's red wagon, now also well speckled with white, as was everything else within twenty feet of the gazebo.

"Okay," Retch said. "But be careful you don't get hit by a car in the dark. That's the only bike I've got."

"It *is* pretty dark," Mr. Sweeney said. "Better get me my flashlight out of the toolbox, Retch."

Retch and I flopped down on the grass and watched his father ride off toward the lake, an eerie white figure that seemed to glow in the dark, the beam of the flashlight bobbing about, the knees splayed out and pumping up almost to the shoulders. He looked like a giant albino grasshopper. We laughed.

It was one of those lazy warm August nights in which men in their undershirts sat on front porches watering their lawns with a hose, teenage boys slouched in clusters around their cars at the Dipsy Queen Drive-in, and giggly girls strolled home after the early show at the Pandora movie theater.

All this mundane tranquillity was starting to get on our nerves. So the screams and shrieks erupting into the night no more than two blocks away came as a welcome surprise. They were wonderful screams and shrieks, edged with just the right amount of terror and hysteria. Retch and I leaped up, ready to partake of the excitement.

"Maybe it's the Flashlight Man," I said.

"Yeah," Retch said. "If he comes this way, let's tackle him. We'll be heroes!"

Suddenly, we glimpsed the glowing-white figure of Mr. Sweeney pedaling furiously across the lower end of the park.

"There goes Popper!" Retch shouted. "Man, he's really moving! He must be chasing the Flashlight Man!"

The wail of a police siren blended in with the screams and shrieks, and a dozen dogs joined the chorus with some off-key harmonizing. Seconds later the town's police car came roaring up the street next to the park, all its lights flashing and its spotlight darting among the trees and bushes. The spotlight passed over Retch and me, and then darted back. The patrol car slid to a stop. Buster Cobb and Sonny Mack, the town police force, waved us over.

"The Flashlight Man's been spotted," Sonny said. "He just rode through the park on a bike. You boys see which way he went?"

We were stunned. "That was Popper!" Retch blurted out. "It was my father!"

Now the policemen looked stunned. "No!" said Buster. "I don't believe it! Herb Sweeney is the Flashlight Man?" He turned to me. "You know anything about this, Pat?"

"N-no," I stammered, because it had never occurred to me that Mr. Sweeney might be the Flashlight Man. Here he had been right within our grasp all the time, and we hadn't known! Lacking any other useful information, I added, "We just watched Mr. Sweeney paint his gazebo."

"Good gosh, this is worse than I thought!" Sonny gasped.

"That's a gazebo, you idiot," Buster said, pointing to the little building.

Retch then explained how his father had painted the gazebo wearing only his swimming trunks and then had ridden down to the lake to wash off.

Scarcely had he finished when Mr. Sweeney came pedaling wildly out of a side street chased by three men in their undershirts. He easily pulled away from them, his pumping knees a whitish blur up around his ears. Retch and I and the policemen stared silently after him, until Mr. Sweeney cut a sharp left into a dark alley. From off in the distance, we heard a shout: "There he goes! After him!" Car engines roared to life and tires screeched from abrupt acceleration.

Buster scratched the stubble on his chin. "Well, I guess it's just a case of mistaken identity. Herb Sweeney obviously ain't the Flashlight Man. Let's go get some coffee, Sonny."

Later that night, Retch and I were lying in our sleeping bags on the Sweeney lawn when Mr. Sweeney came wobbling into the yard on Retch's bike. Somehow he had eluded his pursuers and made it to the lake. He seemed to have aged considerably since we last saw him. Most of his paint was washed off, except for a faint residue that gave him an unnatural pallor. Under the porch light, his hair still looked wet. He stopped on the porch and stared at us long enough to make us uneasy. Then a shot rang out. Retch and I both jumped, even though we knew Mr. Sweeney had no place to conceal a gun. But it was only the screen door banging shut behind him. Parents can get on your nerves.

"It really would have been something if your father had turned out to be the Flashlight Man," I said to Retch.

"Yeah," Retch said. "I'm sorta glad he isn't, though. Popper's weird enough as it is."

The Flashlight Man was never caught, nor even seen again. Several years later another crime was committed in our town, but, as far as I know, Mr. Sweeney wasn't even a suspect. I guess he had learned his lesson.

THE FLY

I have long known that the employees most informed about the inner workings of a business or institution are the janitors. After everyone else has gone home for the day, the janitors move quietly and efficiently through the empty offices, sweeping, mopping, dusting, snooping.

In the unlikely event I ever become president of a company, my first order of business will be to promote the janitor to executive vice president. Then I'll call him into my office and say, "All right, Herb, I want you to tell me what's going on in the company. Care for a drink before we begin? I think I have a bottle of Scotch around here someplace."

"Lower left drawer of your desk," Herb will reply. "Right behind your box of El Puffo cigars, which, I might add, are excellent."

I am something of an authority on the janitorial

profession, having swept my way through four years of college. By graduation, I had cleaned and snooped every building on campus. Janitoring was an education in itself, and my only regret is that I didn't barter some university secrets for a full professorship. As the only tenured sophomore on the faculty, I might have had more luck with girls.

My first janitorial assignment was in a creepy old science building. To an English major, all science buildings are creepy, but this one was creepier than most. It housed an abundance of icky things: a container occupied by a mass of ugly little beetles working diligently to clean the flesh off skeletons; cages filled with thousands of flies buzzing angrily over not being able to get out and annoy people; a dissection room where jars of pickled pink things lined the shelves, a human skeleton dangled unhappily from a metal hanger, and ominous stainless-steel coolers lined the walls beneath grotesque charts of persons wearing not only no clothes but no skin. Yuck!

My first night on the job, Phil and Steve, the other two student janitors, took me on a tour of the building. I gave a small shudder as we looked in on the beetles box. "This is the creepiest thing I've seen yet," I said.

"Really?" Phil said. "That means you haven't met Raymond."

"Raymond?"

"Yeah. Raymond's our boss—the head janitor of Boris Karloff Science Building."

"What's so creepy about him?"

"Among other things, he lurks. You'll be cleaning

out a room and suddenly you'll see Raymond standing off in a corner, lurking. Makes your skin crawl."

We moved on to a departmental office. Steve pointed to a box of chocolates on a secretary's desk. "Always remember to exercise caution in your foraging," Steve said.

"Foraging?" I said.

"Yeah. It's the student janitor's version of living off the land. Secretaries are always leaving goodies out on their desks—candy, cookies, nuts. It's our belief that they are responding to a deep psychological urge to share them with us. On the other hand, there is a remote possibility that the secretaries intend these goodies solely for their own consumption. Therefore, in an effort to avoid hostilities between secretaries and student janitors, it is best if you sample the goodies in such a way that the foraging goes undetected. Do I make myself clear?"

"We don't want to get caught stealing goodies?"

"Correct."

Steve then demonstrated his goody-snitching technique, lifting one edge of the lid of the chocolate box slightly and peering through the crack. He explained that he was looking for a booby trap. I laughed. "No joke," Steve said. "Also, in the case of chocolates, make sure the one you select hasn't been tampered with. A secretary over in Sociology loaded a massive charge of chocolate-flavored laxative into a choice morsel and almost wiped out Charlie Fisk."

"That's terrible," I said.

"Yeah. And poor Charlie wasn't even the one who

ate it. He was just an innocent bystander. So be on your guard."

Later that evening, I met Raymond. Only a few years older than I, the head janitor was a pudgy, pasty fellow in bib overalls who obviously treasured his power over three impoverished student janitors. His piggish little eyes shone with the happy and sadistic malice often found in persons given authority far in excess of their intelligence.

"So, this is what they sent this time," he sneered at me by way of greeting. "Probably don't know one end of a broom from the other."

"The big end goes on the floor," I said. "Did I get it right?"

"Oh ho!" Raymond replied. "I see I got me another wise guy to go with the other two. Well, I'm going to be watching you, and I better not find a speck of dust in any of the rooms you clean. Just for smarting off, you can clean the floor that's got the room with all them caged flies." Raymond allowed himself a shudder. "Flies give me the willies ever since I saw that movie *The Fly*, the one with Vincent Price in it. Guy got turned into a fly! Ugh! Nasty! Hope you enjoy cleaning the fly room."

Whatever his other shortcomings, Raymond proved true to his threats. He hounded me constantly from then on, and Phil and Steve didn't make out much better. Raymond *was* creepy, too. I would be cleaning an office and all at once the short hairs on my neck would snap to attention. I'd glance around and there would be Raymond in a shadowy corner, watching, lurking, smirking.

"Raymond's really got me spooked," Phil said one night. "This guy is too weird. I feel this terrible urge to take a shower in carbolic acid every time he gets within five feet of me."

"But what can we do?" I said.

"I don't know," Phil said. "We need to find something to keep him occupied so he stops his lurking. My nerves can't stand it."

A few nights later Raymond came up with yet another chore for me. "I just got orders that someone on this crew has to lower the flag on the campus tower every night."

"Can't be me," I said. "I hate heights."

"Good," Raymond said. "You're it then."

Lowering the flag required me to climb straight up a hundred-foot steel ladder fastened to an inside wall of the tower. One slip and I would plummet to the concrete floor below. I didn't really mind, though, because I'd always enjoyed climbing. After lowering and folding the flag, I took a few moments to look out over the campus and enjoy a few moments free from the lurking presence of Raymond. I watched the tiny figures of harried students scurrying in and out of the library, riding bikes across the mall, chatting in groups outside the Student Union Building, and hunching over their desks in their dorm rooms. Dorm rooms! Apparently, the campus authorities were unaware that from the vantage point of the tower a person could see right into the upper-story windows of a women's dorm, a Peeping Tom's dream come true! Naturally, I was appalled.

Upon returning to the janitor's room, I complained to Raymond. "I hate this job. My hands get so sweaty I could lose my grip on the ladder and fall and go splat all over that concrete floor."

"So you go splat," Raymond said. "I don't see the problem. There just ain't no way you're going to get out of lowering the flag. That's it. I don't want to hear no more about it."

"Okay," I said. "Oh, by the way, did you know that it's possible to see right into the windows of a women's dorm from the top of the tower? If some sleazy, slimy pervert ever got access to the tower, I'm sure he'd have a field day."

"All right, all right, stop your whining," Raymond said. "If you hate climbing the tower so much, I guess I'll have to lower the flag myself."

Although I never expected to find any redeeming qualities in Raymond, he soon demonstrated a profound sense of patriotism, or so I assumed from the fact that it took him an hour or more every night just to lower and fold the flag.

I expected to be congratulated by my fellow janitors for providing us with some relief from Raymond, but Phil and Steve were both shocked.

"Don't you realize what you've done?" Phil said. "You've allowed that creepy pervert to violate the privacy of the women's dorm! The very least you could have done is turn the job over to me. Sure, I'm a pervert, but at least I'm not creepy."

I soon drifted into a comfortable routine of janitoring: sweep sweep, dust dust, snoop snoop. Out of the old American belief that it's wrong to steal, I made every effort to resist foraging. But one night my conscience was pinned to the mat by a can of mixed nuts on a secretary's desk. Phil was sick, and I was cleaning one of his floors, one where he had apparently been foraging excessively. I decided that the secretary wouldn't mind my liberating a measly nut or two for the purpose of easing the hunger pangs of a famished student. Forgetting Steve's warning about booby traps, I popped off the can's lid, and a spring-loaded rubber snake shot out and arrested several of my vital functions. To further complicate matters, the snake sailed all the way across the room and hid under a piece of furniture. It took me nearly an hour to find the thing and compress it back into the nut can. Foraging was not without its wear and tear on the nervous system, largely because of the secretaries' immaturity, as evidenced by their childish practical jokes.

The icy winds of winter eventually snuffed the flame of Raymond's patriotism. He was soon back to lurking, and I was soon back to lowering the flag. (I heaved a sigh of relief upon discovering that even on the top floor of the dorm, the women were closing their window blinds at night.) As winter tightened its grip on the campus, the lives of the student janitors seemed to alternate between the twin horrors of study and work. To introduce a little excitement into our boring existence, we began to plot little practical jokes to play on Raymond.

Phil and I decided to first test out a prank on Steve to see what bugs needed to be worked out before pulling it on the head janitor. We unscrewed half the light bulbs in the dissection room, leaving a large area in shadow. On the night of the experiment, I arrived at the test site too late to assist. Phil had gone ahead without me. By the time I got there, Phil was hooking an arm back onto the skeleton, and Steve was standing ramrod straight with his back to us. I got the feeling Steve might be a little disgusted that we would use him to test out a prank.

"How'd it go?" I asked Phil.

"Okay," Phil said. "Steve was sweeping that dark corner, when the skeleton reached out and grabbed him by the neck."

"So it worked pretty well?"

"Nothing spectacular," Phil said. "No screams or anything. Anyway, it's getting late. Why don't you go get a hand cart, and we'll stand Steve on it and wheel him down to the faculty lounge and see if a cup of hot coffee won't limber him up enough to finish cleaning the lab."

Phil decided not to pull the skeleton-arm trick on Raymond, because, as he said, it might prove fatal. That would leave only Steve and me to clean the whole building.

We thought of dozens of practical jokes to pull on Raymond, but none of them ever seemed to work out. Then one night I was sweeping up the fly room, when an idea occurred to me. I got a hose from the supply room and ran it up into one of the cages of flies, who responded by increasing their volume of buzzing to a deafening hum. Pulling the other end of the hose after me, I crawled under a nearby desk to await Raymond's inspection tour. The head janitor arrived shortly, muttering irritably to himself as he checked for dirt and dust.

"What's this?" he muttered. "The fool left his cart outside the door, and his broom's still here. Where'd he go?" He yelled out my name, or one of the names he frequently applied to me. I spoke into the hose in a high squeaky voice. From the cage of flies came the tiny pathetic plea: "Help me! Help me!"

After Raymond's departure, I removed the hose from the cage and put it away. Somehow the handle on my broom had been snapped in two and a chair knocked over, and there were some rubber traction marks on the linoleum, but no great damage had been done. Oh, I nearly forgot the scratches on the door, where Raymond had tried to claw his way through before remembering to turn the doorknob. Apparently, Raymond had become entangled in my janitor's cart, because I found it tipped on its side, halfway down the hall, with wastepaper scattered hither and yon and even still fluttering out of the air. There was no sign of Raymond.

The next day Raymond asked for and was granted a transfer to another building. His replacement arrived that evening. He lined his three charges up in the janitor room and walked back and forth in front of us. "I don't know what happened here last night, but I understand from my friend Raymond that you're a bunch of wise guys. Well, don't think you can pull any funny stuff on me. I'm gonna be watching you every minute. I find a speck of dust or dirt anywhere, I'm gonna chew you up and spit you out. Now, any questions?"

"Just one," I said.

"What's that?"

"You ever see that movie *The Fly*?"

MEAN GIFTS

Why is it so often assumed we outdoorsmen are totally lacking in sophistication and good taste? Every Christmas, Father's Day, and birthday we become the recipients of such gifts as ties decorated with leaping bass, gigantic belt buckles engraved with moose heads, table-lamp bases in the form of huge shotgun shells, toilet seats of clear resin embedded with assorted game sign, and so on. Sure, we get plenty of neat gifts like these, but also a lot of tasteless stuff, too.

Some gifts are downright disgusting. A fishing journal, for example, is one of the worst things to give an angler. I once knew a man who enjoyed a sterling reputation for honesty and integrity. One day his wife gave him a fishing journal, which contained designated spaces for species of fish caught, quantity, size, lure/bait, date, place and time, and notes. Melvin was delighted with the journal and rushed right out to catch a fish to record in it.

He caught an eight-inch perch off the city dock using a worm for bait, and then raced back home to make the first entry in his fishing journal. Under *Species*, he penciled in "Yellow Perch," under *Size*, "8 inches," under *Lure/Bait*, "worm," and so on. When he had completed the entry, he sat there smiling with satisfaction, thinking how much fun it would be to let his friends read through the journal and take note of all the wonderful catches he made over the year.

It's just too bad, he thought, that the first entry in his new fishing journal had to be a perch rather than a game fish. How much better it would have been if the fish were a trout, a rainbow, say. He felt a mild depression coming on. It would certainly be easy enough to take the day off and go out to the river and catch a rainbow to use for the first entry. On the other hand, he couldn't afford the time at the moment, but it was an absolute certainty he would catch a nice rainbow if he did go out to the river. Considering that certainty, he wondered whether it was necessary actually, physically, to go out to the river, when he was so short of time, anyway? After thinking about it a moment, he erased "Yellow Perch" and wrote in "Rainbow Trout." That looked much better. It felt good, too. Still, the fish was on the small side. What would it hurt if he added a few inches? He erased the "8 inches," and wrote in "18 inches."

As Melvin told me later, he felt not the slightest

guilt at making these minor changes. Indeed, he could not help but compliment himself on his restraint. There was nothing to prevent him from stretching the fish out to twenty-four or even thirty inches, but he had limited himself to a modest eighteen. If he wanted to be greedy, he could have made it a world's record, but he was a man not given to excesses. And he allowed himself only that one fish, when he could as easily have caught his limit. He made one more tiny change, replacing "Worm" under *Lure/Bait* with "#14 Renegade fly," followed by a note that he had tied the fly himself, which was certainly within the realm of possibility if he ever had the time to learn fly tying. His first entry completed, Melvin closed and shelved his new fishing journal, thoroughly pleased with it and himself.

Now Melvin says he wishes he had never heard of a fishing journal, let alone owned one. "You write in a bogus entry or two and the first thing you know you can't stop," he whines. "Halfway through the journal, I was doing three or four blue marlin a week and an occasional swordfish, all world-class, and I've never even been on the ocean. After a while you don't even bother to go fishing. You just sit in a corner writing big fish into your journal day after day. It's addictive!" Before long he applied the same method to filling out other forms, including his income tax, which explains why Melvin is now doing three to five at Leavenworth. It's kind of sad, when you think about it.

How-to books with the word *Simple* in the title can be disastrous for an outdoorsman. Let's say he receives a book titled *Outboard Motor Overhaul for the Simpleminded*. A book with that title is going to make this guy think even he can actually overhaul an outboard motor, even though he's one of those people who refer to a pair of pliers as "a squeezer." He grabs his book and rushes out to the garage. Within minutes the floor is covered with outboard parts, the big spring that rewinds the starter cord has sprung out and got him by the neck, and electrical current is arcing from his head to a cold water pipe. "Hand me my squeezer, quick!" he yells at his hysterical wife and weeping children. "And read me Chapter Four again, this time real slow."

My friend Retch Sweeney received a book titled *Rod Building Made Simple* for Christmas. Three days later, he had to be surgically removed from a three-foot graphite rod blank. Stubb Hinkle was given *Simple Chainsawing* and cut up three pine trees, a picnic table, a plastic wading pool, and a 1983 Toyota pickup before he found the off switch. These examples indicate why how-to books should come with titles like *Virtually Impossible Electrical Wiring for Your Boat* or *Fly Tying Exclusively for the Mentally and Dextrously Gifted*. Then we outdoorsmen wouldn't feel obligated to read and do them. It would make life a lot simpler.

Along with gross gifts, disgusting gifts, and dangerous gifts are mean gifts. When I was a kid, my parents were always giving me mean gifts: socks,

underwear, sensible things. Sometimes they'd give me
a gift I'd already had for three years.

"Hey, my old bike!" I'd exclaim.

"Yes," my mother would say. "We sneaked it
away and painted it. Like the color?"

"Who wouldn't? Same as the garage!"

Sometimes they would take an ordinary mean gift
and turn it into a terrifically mean gift through the
magic of packaging. I'd gleefully tear open an electric-
train box and find a set of long underwear inside. "Hey,
my old underwear!" I'd say.

"Like the new red patches I sewed on?"

"Great! By the way, where's the train?"

"Your cousin Delmore has it."

I had a rich aunt back East who every Christmas
would send me several neckties, although I'm sure she
didn't intend them to be mean gifts. She probably
thought I had a suit. I didn't even have a neck. The ties,
properly knotted, did make a rather nice sled-dog har-
ness, at least until my sled dog chewed them up.

For firewood, many people in our community
burned mill ends, the short pieces sawed off the ends of
boards. The mills gave them away free. For a few dollars, you could hire a man with a dump truck to haul
enough mill ends to build a three-bedroom house and
heat it all winter. Mill ends made wonderful play blocks.
We kids spent endless hours constructing forts and other
structures out of them. Our playing with mill ends
didn't escape the notice of parents. When the truck came
rumbling in with a load for the woodshed, parents

would sing out, "Here comes Santa Claus!" I was ten years old before I realized Santa drove a sleigh and not a dump truck.

I have tried to keep the tradition of mean gifts alive for my own children and grandchildren, but it's pretty expensive, mostly because of my wife, Bun. When one of my grandsons opens an electric-train box with a suit of long underwear inside, there had better be an electric train in close proximity, and not over at his cousin's. Takes a lot of fun out of it for me. My own father used to get a kick out of stuffing my stocking with rotten potatoes and kindling sticks, "because that's what Santa gives to bad little boys." I knew, of course, that it was my dad who had put the potatoes and sticks in my stocking, but I didn't mind. It made for an equitable arrangement: He saved money and I got to be bad. I've tried to work out this arrangement with my grandchildren, but they don't seem to get the point. "Thanks for the rotten potatoes and kindling," they say. "Now where's the Nintendo?"

One of my favorite mean gifts for a ten-year-old is a savings bond that matures on his eighteenth birthday. The kid had been counting off the days until Christmas; now he has to count off the years until he can "open" his present. Savings bonds are the modern equivalent of the sensible gift.

I recently gave one of my grandsons a huge box of mill ends for his birthday, and all the rest of the family was horrified that I could still be so mean. I personally thought it was a pretty good joke to play on the little tyke, who spent all morning trying to figure out where to put in the batteries. But the joke backfired. The mill ends are now his favorite toy. For his next birthday, I guess I'll have to play it safe and go with the savings bond.

SNAKE

The garage at my cabin has a single layer of concrete blocks for a foundation. The wall doesn't quite cover a block at one corner, leaving part of a cinder block hole exposed. A couple of summers ago, while I was putting up a shelf in the corner, I dropped a nail. When I bent over to pick it up, a snake stuck its head out of the hole in the concrete block. I was mildly surprised, of course, not expecting to find a snake in my garage, let alone in one of my concrete blocks.

My wife, Bun, came running out of the garage. "What in heaven's name happened?" she yelped. "Are you hurt?"

"Just a little whiplash," I said, rubbing the back of my neck.

"Well, why on earth did you scream out that awful word? I thought you had smashed your finger with a hammer."

Bun tends to exaggerate. I certainly did not scream, and the so-called "awful word" wouldn't even make the standard list of words shouted when you smash your finger with a hammer. The truth is I'm rather fond of snakes as individuals, although I certainly wouldn't want to attend one of their conventions.

"It was nothing, really," I said. "Actually, it's kind of cute. Squat down here and look at the hole in this concrete block."

Bun smiled. "What? I bet there's a chipmunk hiding in there."

"Even better," I said. I tapped on the block with my hammer, and the snake stuck its head out. Bun shot into the air like a Patriot Missile. After gaining enough altitude to maneuver, she performed some rather nice aerial acrobatics, although I didn't care much for the audio portion. It had somehow slipped my mind that she is one of those people who go absolutely bonkers at the sight of a snake. She stormed out of the garage in a rage, as though the whole incident were my fault and not the snake's. The snake and I looked at each other and shrugged. At least, I shrugged. I'm sure the snake would have shrugged, too, if he'd had any shoulders.

I told the snake he had better leave while the leaving was good, but he ignored my advice and retracted back into what he now obviously regarded as his private concrete block. Now that I knew that the snake was in residence, he no longer startled me. He soon revealed himself to be a curious fellow, for a snake anyway, and seemed to take an interest in my shelf construction, as if he himself were running short of storage space and might want to build some of his own.

Once the shelves were completed, I went to work outside, excavating dirt for a concrete ramp to the garage. One day the snake came slithering out of the garage to watch that work, too. The poor little beast must have been starved for entertainment. If I was late getting to work in the morning, he would be out there waiting for me, looking at his watch, as if he had me on salary. Now that he knew me better, he started criticizing my work, from time to time darting out his little forked tongue in an expression of disdain, as though he were some kind of expert on garage ramps.

"I don't have to take that from a snake," I'd tell him.

It gets a little lonely out at the cabin, and I guess that's why I started talking to the snake. Our discussions were totally one-sided, of course, so I had to assume what his response to one of my comments might be and speak it for him. Once at dinner, I mentioned to Bun a particularly witty thing the snake had said to me that day, which, in retrospect, I realize probably wasn't a good thing to mention.

"That stupid snake gets more conversation out of you than I do," Bun said.

"Well, if you would come out and lie on the ground next to my diggings, I'd talk to you, too," I replied.

The snake seemed strangely intelligent, not that you'd want him to make out your income tax or anything like that. I suppose I felt flattered that he showed an interest in my activities, something I can't say about most of the people I know. He seemed happy just to be around me, never asked for anything more than my company, and no doubt considered it an expression of affection that I didn't try to kill him. That's my idea of a solid relationship.

The snake obviously had formed an attachment to me, which I found oddly pleasing, although I didn't much care for the idea of bonding with a snake. After the ramp to my garage was completed, the snake started following me about whenever I was out in the yard. I'd glance back, and here would come the snake, slithering along after me. It was sort of like having a dog—a long, very low dog. I wondered if I could teach it tricks. Maybe I could build a little bicycle and train the snake to ride it. I imagined having visitors over and the snake riding up on its bicycle, and somebody screaming "Snake!" and somebody else hitting it with a stick and saying, "Man, I hate snakes!" That's just the way some people are about snakes. So I didn't build the bicycle, even though it would have been fairly easy—one handlebar, one pedal.

One day I decided to rearrange some of the plumbing under the cabin. The access hole to the crawl space had shrunk since I'd built the cabin ten years ago, which is what happens when you build with green lumber. (Bun has a different theory, but it's too ridiculous even to mention.) In any case, I managed to squeeze through the hole and then crawled about looking at the various pipes. After banging my head a few times on floor joists, and sucking in a few spider webs and possibly some spiders, it occurred to me that this was a job for our local handymen, Albert and his son, Lester. I turned to crawl back to the access hole, and there was the snake. He had slithered in right behind me, his eyes sparkling and full of interest in my new undertaking.

"I got bad news for you, sport," I said. "This job is beyond my scope. I have to bring in some professionals."

The snake looked disappointed but didn't say anything.

"Tell you what, though," I went on. "You can stay down here and watch the pros work if you want, and eat some of these spiders while you're waiting." That seemed to please the snake.

"Will you stop talking to that snake!" Bun yelled from the kitchen above. "You're starting to make me nervous!"

The next morning Albert and Lester arrived in their old pickup truck with a box of serious-looking tools. They both wore faded bib overalls in the shape of a watermelon. I thought I might have to grease Albert and the boy to get them through the access hole. They moved in the slow, ponderous, deliberate manner of men who knew their business and that they're being paid by the hour.

"Now, what you want done here is for us to install a pipe on your plumbing so you can drain your entire system from outside the cabin when you close it up for the winter, is that right?" Albert said.

"Right," I said. "I hate climbing under there every fall to drain the water. The worst part is all the spiders. Spiders give me the creeps." I realized instantly that I had made a mistake.

"Spiders! Ha!" Albert chortled. "A grown man like you, afraid of spiders. Well, if that ain't just like you city folk! You hear that, Lester? Man's afeard of spiders!"

"Afeard of spiders!" Lester guffawed.

"I'm not exactly afeard of spiders," I said. "I just don't like the crawly things. The only reason I mentioned it is I thought the two of you might find it amusing."

"We surely did that," Albert said, slapping me on the back. "Lester, go fetch the toolbox and those lengths of pipe. Man's paying us by the hour to do plumbing, not to stand around jawing."

"Right, Pa," Lester said, still chortling. He oozed off in the direction of the truck with all the speed of a tree adding growth rings.

Albert went headfirst into the access hole, which squeezed his fat back into a rounded mass toward the lower half of his overalls. Then he somehow sucked the fat through a little at a time, until he was fully in the crawl space. Lester followed him under the cabin, using the same technique. I supposed it was something they taught at the School for Fat Handymen.

"Afeard of spiders!" I heard Lester yelp.

"Yep!" cried Albert. "These city folk do crack me up."

I sat outside the access hole, listening to the sounds

of work being done, or what I judged to be the case from all the grunting and banging.

"Mighty tight squeeze down here," Albert growled. "If I'd knowed it was going to be this tight, I'd of jacked up my rate. Shine that light over here, Lester, while I get this pipe loosened up. There. Now, I need something to tie her up with. I seen a length of rope around here someplace."

"There it is, Pa. Hold the light a second and I'll toss it to YOUAEEEIIIIIIII! SNAKE! SNAAAAAKE!"

"Stop your durn foolin', Lester, there ain't no . . . SNAKE! GIT THAT SNAKE OFFEN MEEEE!"

My impression was that both Albert and Lester leaped up and started to run for the access hole, which wasn't a good idea, because the crawl space scarcely exceeds three feet in height. I'm not sure whether they actually moved the cabin on its foundation or whether it was merely an illusion created by the excitement of the moment. Lester came clawing his way half out of the access hole. The expression on his face could have been put on poison bottles to frighten off children. Then something grabbed him and dragged him back beneath the cabin, his fingernails leaving scratches across the wood framing. A half second later, Albert plunged through the hole, threatening to take out the entire wall. Forgetting about technique, he squeezed most of his fat down around his ankles and then popped it through like a cork from a bottle.

Once escaped from the crawl space, Albert and Lester danced around shaking like two washing machines with off-center loads.

"Burrrr! You got a snake down there!" Albert cried, shuddering at the very word. "One thing I can't stand is snakes!"

"You fellas afeard of snakes?" I said. "Well, by jove, I'll just crawl down there and get the little devil. You men stand clear when I bring him out."

"Stand clear?" Lester said. "You don't have to worry none about that. I'm going to be in the truck!"

"Me too," said Albert. "And the truck's going to be doing sixty miles an hour toward home!"

So each fall I still have to crawl under my cabin to drain my water system, but I wait until it's cold enough that the spiders have holed up for the winter. The snake still shows up each summer, but since the crawl space incident, he treats me with a sort of reserved detachment, as if I had somehow deliberately offended him. We haven't exchanged a word in more than two years.

SCORE ONE
FOR THE PINKY

Have you ever wondered where the little toggles attached to the bims on zitflangs come from? Well, you are not alone. Many Americans have never wondered the same thing, which tells you something about the sorry state of curiosity in this country.

I once worked in the public relations department of a firm that manufactured the world's entire supply of bim toggles. It was a relatively easy job, since my primary responsibility was to satisfy the public's curiosity about our product. No doubt you've heard the classic slogans I dreamed up for the company: "We toggle your bims!" and "If your bims haven't been toggled by us, they haven't been toggled!"

Although the bim toggle business is tame enough, my boss, Melvin R. Wiggens, was frenetic and insecure, always rushing hither and yon, worrying about this and that, and generally getting on everyone's nerves, particularly mine.

One day Wiggens charged into my office, surprising me in the act of analyzing a magazine centerfold for purposes of market research. Because Wiggens knew little about market research, he didn't realize that it is customarily conducted in the posture of sprawling back in a swivel chair with one's feet propped on a desk.

"Usually, I read only the articles in this magazine," I explained, "but just today I discovered the publication contains this rather distasteful centerfold. In my view, Mr. Wiggens, it would be disastrous for us to advertise bim toggles in such a publication. Furthermore—"

"Shut up," Wiggens snapped, "and put down that nasty magazine and magnifying glass. I have an important assignment for you."

"Gee," I said, "this is a rather bad time. A ground swell of curiosity about bim toggles seems to be rising, and I'd better get right on top of it."

"Forget that. This is a major crisis, and you're the only man in the company who can deal with it."

"Well, since you put it that way . . ."

"Here's what it is," Wiggens said in a tone that could only be described as whiny. "President T. T. Taggart of the parent corporation is flying into town next week to inspect the plant, and he's indicated that he wants to take some time off to go fishing while he's here. You're the only fisherman in the PR department. Your assignment: Take Mr. Taggart fishing. And if I may offer a word of advice?"

I nodded.

"Don't blow it!"

"Surely," I said, catching a bit of Wiggens's panic, "you don't mean Terrible Taggart, old T. T. himself!"

"I do indeed. And I'll not listen to lame excuses from you if the old man doesn't catch fish."

"But fishing is awful around here right now."

"Then take him someplace where it isn't awful. Got it?"

"Got it."

That evening after work I hightailed over to Kelly's Bar & Grill, the watering hole of local sportsmen and other wildlife, to confer with my cronies in the feeble hope that they might come up with a plan for extracting me from my predicament.

"What happens if this Taggart fellow don't catch no fish?" Retch Sweeney asked.

"I'll be out of a job, that's what," I replied.

"Now tell me the bad part." Retch himself was trying to get listed in the *Guinness Book of World Records* for the longest time between jobs.

"That is the bad part," I said. "I need this job."

"In that case, I got an idea. Why don't we take old Taggart up to Skookum County? You can always catch fish up there."

I pondered the suggestion a moment. Not bad, really. "That might work," I said, "but we'd have to stay out of the bars. You know that fracas we got into with those loggers the last time we were up there. We were lucky to escape with our lives!"

"Ha! You call that a fracas? Why, we was just havin' a little fun. You don't think them fellas I was playin' poker with actually got upset 'cause I won that big pot with three aces, do you?"

"As I recall, they were a little disturbed by the fact there were two other aces showing. Three and two adds up to five aces."

"Oh, sure, bring arithmetic into it. So what do you think about haulin' this Taggart up to Skookum?"

"I think it's a good idea, all right. Probably be an experience Mr. Taggart will never forget."

"You bet," Retch said.

T. T. Taggart turned out to be an imposing individual, well over six feet, with iron-gray hair, a square jaw, and eyes as cold and mean as frosted ice picks. Clearly, here was a man who brooked no nonsense and wasn't all that fond of much else. He certainly didn't give the impression of being your regular fun guy.

Wiggens introduced us, his tongue flicking about a trembling smile. "McManus here will be your fishing guide, Mr. Taggart. I'm sure he has a nice surprise in store for you."

"Flies!" Taggart barked.

Wiggens and I both jumped, thinking we might be drawing them.

"Pardon," I said.

"Flies," Taggart repeated. "I fish only with flies—dry flies—nothing larger than a Number Eighteen. Import them, Fisk's of London." His normal tone of speaking combined a shout and a growl.

"Ah, yes," I said. "Good old Fisk's."

"Know Fisk's, do you? I'm surprised an employee of mine can afford flies from Fisk's."

"Oh, I can't afford them, no, sir! Their catalog. I drool over the flies in their catalog. Say to myself, 'Boy, do I ever wish I could afford flies from Fisk's. Dry flies, of course. Number Eighteens and smaller.' "

"Good. You may be my kind of fisherman after all, one who appreciates first-rate flies. One of my vice presidents last year had the audacity to tie on a Number Ten streamer in my presence, if you can imagine that. Drives a cab now in Pittsburgh."

"Serves the blighter right," I said. "If you'll excuse me for a moment, I have to make a phone call."

I stepped into my office and dialed Retch's number. "Forget the night crawlers," I told him. "We won't be needing them."

"But I just spent all morning digging 'em," he yelped. "I'll be danged if I'm going to dump 'em out!"

"Dump them," I ordered. "Flies only. Itty-bitty flies. Got it?"

"Yeah yeah."

Early next morning, Retch and I picked up Mr. Taggart at his hotel. I was driving my mountain car.

"You expect me to ride in that rattletrap?" Taggart snarled.

"It's all I can afford on my salary," I replied.

"In that case, I like it. It riles me to see one of my employees living too high on the hog."

"High on the hog?" Retch said, chuckling. "Why, ol' Pat here don't even live high on the chicken."

I introduced Retch to Taggart, who regarded my sidekick with ill-concealed distaste.

"What's he doing here?" Taggart asked, jerking a

thumb at Retch, who was sprawled on the backseat chewing a cheap cigar. "I thought you were my guide."

"He's here to pack our gear and tend camp," I explained.

"Hmmmm," Taggart replied. "Well, I guess he seems capable of that. He's certainly big enough."

In the rearview mirror, I could see Retch grinning maniacally, his hands moving in a strangling gesture toward the back of Taggart's neck. I shook my head at him. This was not going to be an easy trip.

We drove off in the direction of Skookum County. Taggart, apparently not one for idle chitchat, settled into a thoughtful silence, while Retch snored loudly in the backseat. It seemed doubtful that I could survive this venture unscathed. I wondered what it would be like, driving a cab in Pittsburgh. Probably not too bad.

A couple of hours later, we reached Skookum County and soon were winding up a logging road that dipped and twisted and turned back on itself and in general did everything but roll over. Taggart sat tensely alert, his nose pressed to the window, and stared down at the river half a mile almost directly below.

"Watch out for that rock!" he shouted. "Ye gods, man, didn't you see that tree in the road! Slow down! Speed up! Easy! Easy! How much longer before we get to the river?"

"About thirty seconds, if our luck don't hold," Retch said. "We're coming to the bad stretch of road."

"The bad stretch! I thought we were already on the— Stop! Stop! There's no road, you fool, there's no road!"

Retch burst out laughing, and even I was mildly amused. Taggart wasn't even looking at the bad stretch yet.

Half an hour later we finally wound down a series of sharp switchbacks and arrived at the river. Retch and I got out and unloaded our gear and pitched the tent.

"Do you think old Taggart's relaxed enough so we can remove him from the car?" Retch said.

"I think so," I said. "I saw him twitch a minute ago."

"Good," Retch said. "I'll grab a screwdriver to pry his fingers loose from the dashboard."

We soon had Taggart sitting in a camp chair with a cool can of beverage clamped in his trembling hand.

"I can't believe it," he whispered hoarsely. "I'm still alive! We actually made it off that road without a single fatality or even injury!"

"I don't know about that," Retch said. "You probably damaged my hearing from all that screamin' you did. But I don't reckon it's permanent."

Taggart glowered at Retch. "I was not screaming! I was merely shouting orders at the fool driver. After suffering through the horrors of that drive in here, I'll tell you one thing."

"What's that, sir?" the fool driver asked politely.

"This had better be the most fantastic fishing I've ever had in my life!"

I studied the river. "Uh, the water seems a little high," I said, recalling that this was one of the favorite lines of fishing guides. "Anyway, here's my plan. Mr.

Taggart and I'll fish upstream, and Retch, you fish downstream."

"Sounds good to me," Retch said. "That way I won't have to listen to . . . !"

I made a throat-cutting gesture. Retch grinned fiendishly and walked off.

Taggart and I fished hard all afternoon without a single strike. Actually, I had a fish on briefly, but managed to shake it loose, before Taggart noticed. Toward evening, we gave up and headed back to camp. Taggart was furious, although I was the one who should have been upset. After all, he wasn't the one who would soon be driving a cab in Pittsburgh.

As he slogged down the trail, Taggart's rage slowly turned to a mood closer to melancholy. "You know, I was really looking forward to some fresh trout fried over an open fire. What are we having for supper by the way?"

"Hamburger Surprise," I said.

"Hamburger Surprise," Taggart repeated, sadly shaking his head.

Retch was already back in camp when we got there. He had a nice fire going and was chopping up more wood for the evening.

"Pretty tough fishing," he said.

"Yeah," Taggart said, flopping into a camp chair with a sigh. "You catch anything?"

"I fished all afternoon with itty-bitty flies and never got a single strike. So then I went to wets."

"Wets!" Taggart growled.

"Still nothing. I figured I'd better head back to

camp, but I wanted a trout for my supper. So I tied on a Number Eighteen Pinky and drifted it down into a nice deep dark hole, and wham bam! Caught these two fat twelve-inch cutthroats one right after another."

Taggart and I stared at the trout Retch gleefully held up.

"I don't suppose you'd consider sharing," I said.

"No way!" Retch said. "You guys catch your own. That's how it works."

"I've never heard of a Number Eighteen Pinky," Taggart said. "Let me have a look at one."

I silently mouthed "No! Don't!" at Retch, but he ignored me. He pulled a can from his vest and extracted a night crawler.

Taggart's eyes first widened in surprise and then narrowed to hard little slits as he stared at the dangling worm. The silence was dreadful. A bird chirped. The fire crackled. The river gurgled.

Taggart slowly rose from his chair. "A Number Eighteen Pinky," he said. "Tie it yourself?"

"You bet," Retch said.

"Got a couple extras?"

"Sure. Here, take my fly book." Retch handed his worm can to Taggart.

"Thanks," Taggart said. He grabbed his rod and headed for the river. Half an hour later he was back with four more fish and a big smile.

That evening we relaxed around the fire, while Retch regaled Taggart with some of his wild tales, and the old man even told a few of his own. He actually seemed to enjoy himself. The next morning, the river was down, and the fish were mad for flies. The chances of my ever driving a cab in Pittsburgh diminished to zip.

On the way home the following day, Retch and Taggart both sat in back and sang "Ninety-Nine Bottles of Beer on the Wall." We stopped by one of the Skookum County bars for lunch, and as usual Retch got into a game of poker with some loggers, while Taggart and I shot a few games of pool. I couldn't help but smile at how well the trip had turned out after all. Terrible Taggart and I were practically buddies. I might even be in for a big promotion. What could possibly go wrong now?

"Three aces beats two pair," Retch said.

THE KELLY IRREGULARS
LEARN TO CRY

I dropped in at Kelly's Bar & Grill the other evening and announced loudly to the Kelly Irregulars, "Hey, guys, guess what? It's okay for men to cry!"

My announcement was greeted by a resounding silence. Kelly, who had stretched his undershirt out from his belly for the purpose of drying a shot glass, stared at me in disbelief. "Who says?" he asked.

"This psychologist on the television, that's who."

"You're putting us on," Retch Sweeney said. "This is another one of your jokes, right?"

"No, it's true," I said. "First you get in touch with your feelings and after that, you cry."

"Why would I want to cry?" Stubb Hinkle said.

"Because it will make you feel good," I said.

"I feel okay now," Stubb said. "As a matter of fact, I feel great. I just won three straight hands of poker."

"Yeah," I said. "But you haven't gotten in touch

with your feelings. After you get in touch with your feelings, you'll feel bad. So then you'll cry. That'll make you feel good."

"I think I'll just skip getting in touch with my feelings," Stubb said. "That way I'll go right from happy to happy. Deal the cards, Sweeney."

"Crying will help you pick up girls," I said.

"So, let's think about this a minute," Stubb said. "Tell me more about this feeling stuff."

"Well, as I understand it, the modern woman is looking to form a relationship with a sensitive man. A man who cries is obviously a man in touch with his feelings and therefore a sensitive man, as opposed to, let's say, a lazy, insensitive, cigar-chomping, poker-playing oaf whose major cultural attainment is comic belching. No offense, Stubb."

"None taken. I guess I could have a go at getting in touch with my feelings. Heck, it's been so long since I've been in touch with a feeling, I'm not even sure where to look for one. But I'm willing to give it a try. A little self-improvement never hurt nobody."

A bunch of the other guys shouted out that they would like to get in touch with their feelings, too.

"Wait a darn minute!" Kelly roared from behind the bar. "I don't want all these elbows to start blubbering like a pack of crybabies. Be bad for business."

"Don't worry," I told Kelly. "This is not the appropriate setting for getting in touch with feelings. What we need to do is go on a camping trip."

"A camping trip?" Retch Sweeney said. "This really is a joke, ain't it?"

"Not at all," I said. I went on to explain how the psychologist on television had taken twenty or so men out on a camping trip. Scarcely a day into the trip, he had them all crying and screaming and beating the ground with sticks, they were so in touch with their feelings. I knew the psychologist was on to something, because I myself had been on camping trips where I'd felt like crying and screaming and beating not only the ground with sticks but some of the other campers as well. Not realizing that I was in touch with my feelings, I had kept these emotions bottled up and never shed so much as a single tear. Afterwards, I went about for weeks being insensitive. Fortunately, nobody seemed to notice. A camping trip obviously was the perfect situation for getting in touch with feelings and learning how to cry.

"We gonna take a psychologist along with us?" Eddie O'Toole asked.

"Naw," I said. "I'll play the part of the psychologist. I took Psych One-oh-one in college."

"That don't seem like much," Eddie said.

"I took it twice."

"Well, okay then!"

The following weekend I rented a van to haul the Kelly Irregulars and our gear to a little campsite far up in the mountains. We pitched our tents and rolled out our sleeping bags next to a tumbling mountain stream. The guys spent the afternoon fly-fishing. It wasn't long before I detected the first sign that one of them had been put in touch with a feeling. Burt Hix returned to camp with tears in his eyes.

"Tell me about it, Burt," I coaxed. "Your feeling had something to do with a recollection of your early relationship with your father, if I'm not mistaken?"

"No," he said, plopping down on a log. "I just hooked the biggest rainbow trout of my life and had it slip off not six inches from the net. Man, that hurts. So near and yet so far."

"Stifle it, Burt," I said sternly. "We're here to learn how to cry, not whine. Now tell me this. Exactly where were you when you hooked that rainbow and what fly were you using?"

That evening, after feeding the guys a sumptuous dinner of my Whatchagot Stew, a rack of wieners, and sand-pit biscuits, I gathered them around the fire to begin my probe of their innermost feelings.

"Any of you guys touched a feeling yet that you would like to tell us about?" I asked.

They looked from one to another, obviously embarrassed. Finally, Pete Boggs hesitantly raised his hand.

"Yes, Pete?" I said encouragingly.

"Gosh, I don't know," he said. "It's just that sitting here around the fire with you fellas reminded me of a camping trip I went on with my father."

"Your father," I said. "Very good. As far as I could determine from the psychologist on TV, fathers are to blame for most of their sons' bad feelings. Once they were put in touch with their feelings, the psychologist's campers claimed they were all messed up emotionally because their fathers hadn't paid enough attention to them. To tell the truth, I couldn't blame the fathers all that much. But go ahead, Pete."

Pete, clearly suffering, related the following. "Well, me and Pop were camped out on the Kootenai River, and Pop cooked dinner over the fire just like you did tonight and afterwards we lay in our sleeping bags looking up at the stars and talking. And I got to thinking about that night, and pretty soon this terrible feeling started welling up inside of me."

"Probably something your father said," I suggested.

"Actually, it was something he cooked. I haven't had indigestion like this since the old man concocted that green hash of his!"

"Wow, that's a relief," Retch Sweeney said. "Here I thought I was in touch with a feeling, and it's only heartburn."

"Would you guys knock it off!" I said. "This is serious business. Now somebody better come up with something cruel his father said or did to him, or there's no nightcap tonight."

Psychologists call this shock therapy. I could see that it was working. Their faces screwed up in intense concentration as the Kelly Irregulars tried to rake up some sins of their fathers.

"Hey, I think I got one!" shouted Stuart Simpson. Everybody applauded and several of the guys slapped Simp on the back. "Way to go, Simp!" Retch said.

"Tell us about it, Simp," I said softly. I could see he was deeply in touch with a feeling, because his eyes were glistening wetly in the firelight. If it wasn't just from the smoke, I figured I had my first crier.

"One day my dad came home and caught me sitting in front of the TV when I was supposed to be out raking the yard," Simp said. "He yelled at me. Then he started ripping up my comic books. I told him I'd run away. He said, 'Great! Write when you get work!' Just like that. So I left home and moved in with a friend and got a job doing janitor work at nights. It hurts."

"That's wonderful, Simp!" I exclaimed. "Absolutely wonderful!"

Simp smiled sadly through his tears, which were actually starting to trickle down his face. The other fellows looked more than a little shaken by the story.

Retch Sweeney cleared his throat. "Gee, your old man was pretty tough on you, Simp. I wish I could come up with a bad feeling like that about my dad. How old were you anyway?"

"Thirty-two."

We all sat there staring silently into the fire, as Simp sniffled and snuffled.

"Simp," I said kindly, "I appreciate your sharing that with us. It must have been painful for you. I know it was painful for me."

"Thanks," Simp said. "Now do we get the nightcap?"

"Yes, indeed," I said. "Hot chocolate for everybody! Break out the marshmallows, boys!"

The Irregulars howled in agony and a couple burst into tears. It was a start.

Just before the icy downpour that night, a wind came up and blew down the tents. The rain turned to snow by morning, and we had to eat cold cereal for breakfast, because we couldn't get a fire going. The men complained because I had used up all the milk on the hot chocolate the night before, and they had to eat their cereal dry. I explained that milk wouldn't have helped dry oats all that much anyway.

"I'm freezing and starving to death," Retch Sweeney moaned. "I say we all pile into the van and drive down to Burt's Roadhouse for hot coffee and sausage and bacon and eggs and stacks of pancakes streaming with butter and syrup."

Upon hearing this, a number of Irregulars sobbed openly and unashamedly as they pleaded with me to head for Burt's.

"No way," I said. "I haven't yet managed to put you guys in touch with your feelings. Besides, the van's out of gas."

At that, all the Irregulars began to cry and scream and run around beating the ground with sticks. It was wonderful. So wonderful in fact, I joined in myself.

Late that afternoon, a forest ranger loaned us enough gas to get back to town. It was a miserable drive. I don't know how many times I had to yell at the Irregulars, "Would you guys shut up! I'm sick to death of your blubbering!"

A mile or so from Burt's Roadhouse, I stopped the van and made everybody take an oath that in the future we would all keep our feelings decently bottled up and never cry in front of another person, unless, of course, it was a really sharp-looking modern woman.

When I got home from the camping trip, my wife,

Bun, met me at the door. "How did it go?" she asked. "You manage to iron out the wrinkled psyches of the Kelly Irregulars?"

"More or less," I said. "But I'm beat. How about cleaning up the van for me and sorting out all the wet gear?"

"No way," she said, pleasantly.

"Please," I said. "Otherwise, I may cry."

"Sorry, bucko," she replied. "I'm going shopping."

So maybe crying doesn't work with all modern women. Still, it was worth a try.

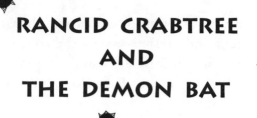

RANCID CRABTREE
AND
THE DEMON BAT

Scarcely had I settled into a patio chair with a can of beverage and some cigars close at hand than the sound of hammering came drifting over my back fence. Well, good, I thought, Felton has taken up building something instead of pestering me. Felton is the eight-year-old rich kid who lives next door and the reason for the fence in the first place. It had been a good three weeks since he had climbed over the fence. Perhaps he was discouraged by the coils of concertina wire I uncoiled along the tops of the boards. The hammering continued for nearly an hour. At last, curiosity got the better of me.

"What are you building over there, Felton?" I called out.

"A ladder," he called back.

A ladder? How odd, I thought, not without a certain sense of foreboding.

Presently, a rather crude ladder was thrust over the top of the fence and rested against the roof of my garden shed. Felton climbed the ladder, stepped off onto the roof, and calmly descended a sloping pile of stacked firewood into my yard.

"You know what?" he said, smiling. "That wire you put on top of your fence to keep burglars out kept me out too. That's why you haven't seen me for three weeks."

"Really?" I said. "I've been wondering about that. I'm sorry, Felton, but I will have to report to your father that you have been using his tools to build a ladder when you're supposed to be watching TV."

"The ladder was Dad's idea. Said it would get me out of the house for a while. He says you remind him of himself when he was a kid."

"Oh he does, does he?"

"Yes. He says you're probably a good influence on me, and I can spend as much time with you as I want."

"What a great guy, your dad. Well, don't just stand there, Felton. Sit down and have a cigar."

"Thanks, but I don't smoke. You know, building that ladder was a lot of fun. You ever build a ladder?"

"Can't say that I have. Anyway, I have to do some work. You see, when I sit here in this chair as though I'm half asleep, well, I'm actually working."

"Yeah, right. Listen, you tell me about one thing you built when you were a kid, and I'll leave you alone."

"Okay, just one thing. Let's see. Well, my friend

Retch Sweeney and I built a kite once. How about that?"

"Naw, that's dumb. I've built kites."

"Sure, from kits your old man bought at a store. But I bet you never built a kite like this one."

As I told Felton, Retch and I were about twelve when we came up with the idea for the wonderful kite. We had already built a kite designed to drop bombs on the tree house of Ronnie Crankshaft, but, due to technical difficulties, we could never get the bombs to drop at the right time, namely when Crankshaft had his head stuck out the window. The bombs had been produced by chickens who had long since died of old age. A direct hit on Crankshaft would have compelled him to live permanently in the tree house, with his parents poking his food up to him on the ends of long poles. Even a near miss would have kept him in the tree house for a couple of weeks, long enough for him to contemplate the folly of committing war crimes against us.

"Too bad we don't have a little person to pilot the kite," I said to Retch. "Then he could release the bombs at just the right moment. What we need is a tiny pilot."

"How about Peewee Thompson?" Retch said.

"Peewee's scared of heights," I said. "We'd have to bind and gag Peewee to get him to pilot one of our kites."

"So what's the problem?" Retch said.

"He'd be bound and gagged, that's the problem," I said. "How could he pilot the kite? Besides, we'd have to build a huge kite to lift even Peewee."

204 THE GOOD SAMARITAN STRIKES AGAIN

We drifted into a thoughtful silence.

"You know what?" Retch said.

"Yeah," I said. "If we built a big enough kite, it could lift one of us! We could drop the bombs on Crankshaft ourselves! Unfortunately, we don't have the kinds of materials we'd need to build a kite that big."

"Hey, maybe we do. My old man bought some long bamboo poles years ago to make some flyrods out of. He was going to split the bamboo and glue it all back together. Pretty weird, huh? He ain't never going to build those rods anyway, so we might as well use the poles. They're light and strong and plenty long enough. And Popper's got a big old lightweight canvas tarp he used to use for camping. We could borrow that. It's all black from smoke but it'd work fine for a kite. Popper never camps anymore anyway."

We went over to the Sweeney house and asked Mr. Sweeney if we could use some of the materials in his garage to build a kite.

"A kite?" Mr. Sweeney said, frowning over the top of his newspaper. "I thought you clowns just built a kite."

"We did," Retch said. "Now we want to build a bigger one."

Mr. Sweeney was silent for a moment, apparently sorting through all the potential problems a kite might cause him. "Oh, all right. See what you can find out in the workshop."

"Thanks, Popper."

We assembled the kite out at my place, a small farm a couple of miles from town. It was remarkably easy to build. Because cutting the canvas to kite shape might bring on one of Mr. Sweeney's attacks of nerves, the symptoms of which consisted mostly of a red face and loud yelling of bad words, we decided it would be best simply to fold the tarp into kite shape. The tail was a bit of a problem, but we eventually solved it by tying old gunnysacks to a rope.

We hung a swing under the cross beam of the kite for the pilot to ride on. As an afterthought, we added a safety belt, actually a dress belt acquired from Mr. Sweeney's closet, but since Mr. Sweeney hardly ever dressed up, he certainly wouldn't miss it for a couple of days. Boxes were taped to the swing ropes to carry bombs. By the end of one day of construction, the kite was completed. It was massive. Now all we needed was enough rope to use for a kite string. The next day, I collected my mother's clothesline and Retch collected his mother's.

"What's a clothesline?" Felton interrupted, right in the middle of my narrative.

"It's an elongated clothes dryer that doesn't require electricity," I explained. "Very modern. Now do you want to hear this story or ask a bunch of stupid questions?"

Anyway, I continued, we decided we didn't have enough clothesline to fly the kite at sufficiently high altitudes, or, to be more specific, out of range of Crankshaft's slingshot. So we stopped by daffy old Mrs. Swisher's, and asked if we could borrow her clothesline. "What for?" she asked, guessing that hanging out wash wasn't one of our normal activities.

"For an aeronautical experiment," I explained.

"Well, all right," she said. "But you bring it back when you're done. And you boys stay away from that smelly old woodsman, Rancid Crabtree. He's in cahoots with demons, you know. He might sacrifice you to the demons."

"Right," I said. The rank old woodsman she spoke of happened to be a good friend of mine, and had taught me a whole bunch of good stuff, some of it so good I was pretty sure my mother didn't want me to know it. If you could stay upwind of Rancid, he was darn good company. He told wonderful stories about when he had been an ace fighter pilot in World War I, a boxing champion, a deep-sea diver, a race-car driver, a trapeze artist in the circus, and I don't remember what-all. A man who had done all that wouldn't have anything to do with demons, for lack of time if nothing else. He now lived in a little shack at the foot of the mountain behind our farm and trapped for a living, mostly skunks, as was evident to anyone passing less than a hundred yards downwind of him.

The path to our testing area for the kite led right past Rancid's cabin. He was sitting on his porch whittling out stretcher boards for his pelts when we went by.

"What in tarnation is thet contraption?" he shouted at us.

"A kite," I explained. It was understandable that Rancid wouldn't recognize it for what it was, because we had it broken down and folded up. "We're going to reassemble it up on the hill above old Mrs. Swisher's house. There's usually a good breeze up there."

"Mighty big kite," Rancid said.

"Yep. This is a human-piloted kite," Retch said. "Pat's going up in it for the test flight."

"Wait a minute," I said. "You said you wanted to fly it first."

"I changed my mind. Why should I have all the fun?"

"Ah better go along and make sure you fellas don't git yersevs kilt," Rancid said. "Ah bet this durn kite of yorn don't even git offen the ground. Ha!"

Half an hour later we were reassembling the kite on the hill above Mrs. Swisher's house. I was glad to see that she wasn't out in her yard. You could never tell what might trigger one of her spells. Catching sight of Rancid standing on the hill above her house was definitely a contender, though.

By the time the kite was assembled, our excitement had reached fever pitch. "I guess I will try it first," Retch said.

"No, I want to," I said.

"It's Popper's bamboo and canvas," Retch said. "So I get to go first." He had me there. A gentle breeze was buffeting the kite about as Retch climbed into the swing and fastened the safety belt. I grabbed the clothesline and pulled it tight. Retch stood at the brink of the hill and waited. Nothing happened.

"Har!" Rancid laughed. "This is the gol-durn stupidest thang Ah ever seed!"

Frankly, I was more than a little embarrassed by the fluttering monstrosity of a kite, with its ridiculous tail of gunnysacks hanging limply from the stern. It was black, ugly, and unwieldy. We had been fools even to think such a thing might fly. As I stood there studying our bizarre creation, the breeze picked up. The canvas billowed out. The kite came to life! I hauled back on the line, and all at once Retch, miraculously zigzagging back and forth, was snatched a good three feet off the ground. The pull of the kite dragged me skidding toward the brink of the hill, but Rancid grabbed the line and helped restrain the pulsating craft. The test pilot watched this brief but frantic activity with a good deal of interest and even solemnity. A few seconds later the breeze died, and Retch drifted gently back to earth.

"Wow! It works!" he cried. "It works! That was great!"

"Wahl Ah'll be," Rancid said. "It do work!"

I took my turn in the kite swing. The wind gusted a bit stronger now, and I soared up a scary five feet before settling back to the hilltop. "Neato!" I yelled, remembering for the first time in two minutes to take a breath.

"Danged if thet don't look like fun," Rancid said. "Maybe Ah should give it a try. Bet it won't lift me."

"Go ahead," I said. "Retch and I'll hold the line."

"Don't mind if Ah do. But you boys take a couple tarns of the line around thet thar tree. Ah don't want to git blowed off into a power line or somethin'. Ha!"

After calmly biting off a chaw of tobacco, Rancid got in the swing and fastened the safety belt. Holding the cross beam of the kite with his hands spread wide, he stood on the edge of the hill, the wind buffeting the great expanse of canvas above him. Retch and I pulled the line taut. The lanky old woodsman waited expectantly, the kite tugging at him. "Ain't gonna work, boys," Rancid said. "Ah is jist too durn heavy fer it. Shucks!"

An hour later Retch and I were headed back down the path toward home.

"Man, what a storm!" Retch said, struggling against the wind. "I ain't never seen one come up so fast before."

"Not this time of year," I said, dodging as somebody's chicken coop bounded by. "Sometimes in March we get winds almost this bad. Your hands still hurt?"

"Yeah. Worst rope burns I've ever had."

"Me too. That ol' clothesline was smoking."

"Well, at least Rancid got some flight time in," I said. "It wasn't our fault he didn't enjoy it."

"Let's stop by Rancid's. He's got some Bag Balm we can rub on our hands. I imagine he'll be cooled down enough by the time he gets back."

Just as we expected, daft old Mrs. Swisher called Sheriff O'Reilley to report the incident. The sheriff knew how peculiar she was, but he liked to humor her. I think he even got a kick out of her fantastic stories. After leaving Mrs. Swisher's, he stopped by Rancid's shack to have a talk with the old woodsman.

"Now, Crabtree, I've warned you about this before," the sheriff said, as Rancid poured him a cup of coffee. "I want you to stop tormenting that poor old

Mrs. Swisher. I've got enough work to do without running out here all the time."

"Me tormentin' her!" Rancid yelped. "It's thet ol' loon what's tormentin' me!"

"Well, I know you did something," the sheriff said. "Whatever it was, she came up with an outrageous tale just to get even. Seems these boys were involved some way, too. Let's see, I've got it here in my notes. Goes something like this:

" 'I heard this terrible ruckus from up on the hill above my house. Well, I went out to see what was happening, and I almost fainted. A huge demon bat had swooped down and snatched up that horrible Rancid Crabtree, and old Crabtree was just screechin' and cussin' for all he was worth. Served him right, him being in cahoots with the devil and all. Anyway, they soared right out over my house, must have been a couple hundred feet high. The wind had come up somethin' fierce, and that bat was darting this way and that. I thought maybe it might drop Crabtree, not bein' able to stomach the smell of him, and come for me. So I grabbed the shotgun and started blasting away. Naturally, I realized I might hit Crabtree, but I figured him for a goner anyway. Well, I ain't much of a shot and didn't come within ten feet of hitting the creature, but I put a good scare into it, I can tell you that. After the first shot, it started flapping those big ugly wings like crazy and flew right back to the top of that hill, fightin' the wind all the way. The bad thing was old Crabtree got loose. A few minutes later, I saw him runnin' down the hill. Almost looked like he was chasin' two boys.

Probably tryin' to catch them to feed to the bat. Be about like him!' "

"That's the craziest tale Mrs. Swisher's come up with yet," the sheriff said. "Not a bit of truth in it, of course. By the way, Crabtree, you look a little shaky. Not coming down with something, are you?"

"It's nothin', sheriff. Maw arms are jist a little knotted up from too much hard work too fast."

"Hard work?" the sheriff said. "I thought you had an aversion to work of any kind, Crabtree."

"Now and agin Ah gits the urge."

I leaned back in my patio chair and blew a smoke ring over little Felton's head, where it hovered for a moment like a halo.

"Gee," he asked, "was Rancid Crabtree really in cahoots with demons?"

"Not really," I said. "Oh sure, he claimed he knew two young demons, but he was always making up ridiculous stuff like that. Retch Sweeney and I spent a lot of time over at his cabin, and we never once saw a single demon or anything that even looked like one. Philosophically speaking, though, I suppose everybody has his own little demon or two. Which reminds me, Felton, isn't it about time you headed home?"

"Okay," he said. "But do you suppose tomorrow we could build a kite big enough for me to pilot?"

"Hey, no problem," I said. "But check with your father first. I wouldn't want him to think I was a bad influence."